Sequins and Sorrow

By

Marty Diamond and Erica Stux

ISBN: 1-4033-0344-4

This book is printed on acid free paper.

1stBooks - rev. 05/15/02

This is a true story, but the names of some individuals have been changed.

Chapter 1

I approached the school building, holding my son Corky's hand, my heart beating with trepidation. Two years of speech therapy had not helped him. He had yet to utter his first word at age five. Would Weaver School be able to bring Corky out of his silent world?

The grounds looked inviting: colorful play equipment fenced in at one end of the building. Corky would like that. The rhythmic motion of a swing always calmed his hyperactivity. He liked a slide also, although the first time I put him on one he had screamed in terror. His little legs now propelled him, two steps to each of mine, past a line of small birch trees that cast spindly shadows on the dark mansard roof, and finally to the main entrance.

I was not prepared for the devastating experience that greeted me inside. Lined up in the corridor were children in wheelchairs, children hooked up to oxygen tanks, children engaged in awkward jerky motions. I couldn't help touching, hugging, or shaking hands with each one, though of course they were total strangers. I was so overwhelmed over what I was seeing, I completely forgot about Corky walking behind me. I wonder what he thought, seeing me in tears as I stopped at each child.

I realized there are so many ways a child can be handicapped: Spina bifida, cystic fibrosis, cerebral palsy, Down's syndrome. All the parents of these children had high hopes for them. All were disappointed. How did they handle their disappointment? Did they develop warm loving feelings for their child nevertheless? Did they feel guilty, angry, embarrassed? Are they overcompensating by indulging their child, letting him get away with unruly, unacceptable behavior? Are they doing the simplest tasks for their child, thus keeping him from learning how to help himself? Did they become hostile to the child, or to the other parent?

Seeing so much collective misery, I ached for all the parents of these children. They must have gone through the same emotional phases that I had: first, denial; then admission that a problem exists; gradual and grudging acceptance of the reality; and finally the last step, which I was just beginning to edge into myself: a determination not to let despair and hopelessness get the best of oneself.

1

Perhaps it was a good thing that I was a single parent. I had the final say about anything affecting Corky, and there was no one to offer contradictory advice, except perhaps the teachers who would be working with him. I had heard of parents whose handicapped child caused continual arguments between them; in some cases it led to divorce. I didn't have to worry about my own family in that respect. They had conveniently pushed my problem out of their consciousness, like the horse thief in one's family who is best forgotten.

Anger then seized me. At least some of these children could think and reason. Their bodies may be defective, but their minds were not. With Corky, however, that wasn't so. His brain damage could possibly be irreversible. On the other hand, did my son really belong here, among all these children that are in worse condition than him? But then I realized he'd be with kind people who would do their best to help him. So from then on, a small yellow bus picked Corky up each morning to take him to Weaver, and returned him in the afternoon.

He was put in a class of about twelve kids. They were given finger paints, clay, and other art supplies to play around with. Listening to music was a frequent activity. The children were taught the importance of getting to their classes on time. Sometimes a class was taken to a roller rink or an ice-skating rink.

The teachers also worked one-on-one with the children, using behavior modification techniques. This procedure involves giving the child a simple command, like "stand up", "pick up the blue block", "point to the red crayon", and giving a small reward, say a potato chip, when the child complied. Usually the very first command is "Look at me." To some extent I followed this procedure with Corky at home, although at first I felt that a child should not be treated like a puppy in need of training. But I saw that the method got results. As Corky got older, I replaced the potato chip rewards with nickels or dimes. Nevertheless, it would be years before Weaver School had any noticeable effect on Corky's behavior, and sometimes I despaired that there would ever be any.

Chapter 2

The birth of Corky presented me with a set of problems that I never knew existed. I had taken such good care of myself during my pregnancy. How could it happen that my baby was born with a handicap?

At an early age I absorbed the fact that my life would not be easy because of the color of my skin. Not only was I "black", but very dark, and within the African-American community there was subtle discrimination against dark-skinned individuals. My mother had told me that when she married my stepfather, his family had asked scornfully "Why you marry her? She too dark!" That was the apparent reason why none of his family with the exception of one brother ever visited us.

Uncles, aunts, and cousins of Mommy's family, on the other hand, visited us frequently. Sometimes one or another of them presented me with a dime or a quarter, and I'd go skipping off to the candy store to spend it, being careful not to trip on the broken and uneven sidewalks that prevailed in our part of town. But on such occasions my younger half-sister always received fifty cents. I chalked it up to the fact that she was light-skinned and therefore more lovable.

The consequences of skin color was underscored when I reached high school. White girls were invited to parties. White girls went out on dates and had steady boyfriends. A few African-American girls had boyfriends, it was true, but there again, it was the light-skinned ones who reaped male attention. I would have liked to be a cheerleader, but those positions were reserved for white girls. I accepted the fact that some doors would always be closed to me.

I was not ready for a problem that did not involve skin color. It was my mother who first sensed something was wrong with Corky.

"He's too calm and quiet for a baby," she said when he was about three months old. "He doesn't smile like a baby should."

I was hurt by Mommy's assertions. I didn't want to admit that my baby could be less than perfect. His daddy was a very handsome man, with chocolate skin and a lazy smile that revealed a row of teeth white and even as piano keys. I had fallen for him hard; whenever he came over, my heart fluttered like a sparrow taking a dust bath. And

3

when he kissed me, my heart did flipflops, like an Olympic gymnast on the balance beam.

When I told John I was pregnant, the news brought on a storm of verbal abuse.

"You tryin' to make me poor?" he yelled. "It's all I can do to pay for the two kids I already got! How could you let yourself get pregnant?"

"But I want a baby."

"You want a baby!" His words came out like machine-gun fire. "Did you ask me? Did you even think of what I want? You ain't nothin' but a thoughtless bitch!"

His tirade continued until he ran out of words. From then on, our life together became an uneasy truce.

I was three months pregnant when he hit me. That was the end of our relationship - or so I thought. I moved from my apartment in Akron, Ohio, to my mother's house in Alliance, a town about 25 miles away, to await the birth of my baby. During that time I saved TV stamps to buy the baby things I would need. The stamps were pasted into a little booklet, and when the booklet was full it could be redeemed for merchandise.

Shabazz Jamal Diamond was born on August 29, 1971, weighing seven-and-a-half pounds. He had an unusual bump on his head, but the nurses told me it was a pressure bump, the result of the forceps delivery, and nothing to worry about.

My younger brother, who was a militant African-American then, came to the hospital and told me, "You've got to name him Shabazz. It's an African king's name, and of course you know it's Malcolm X's assumed name, before he became just Malcolm X."

I thought the name had a nice ring to it, so I agreed. I decided on Jamal for a middle name, after the jazz pianist Ahmad Jamal. Long before the birth, my mother was referring to the baby as Corky. "You and Corky want some watermelon?" she'd ask. Or "You and Corky come along, let's go to the drugstore." So of course Corky became the baby's nickname.

John came to the hospital once to see me and his newborn son. Then he decided he wanted me back. I moved in with him, into a twinplex near Perkins Park in Akron when Corky was about eight months old. I hoped it would work. I still had loving feelings towards him. But he often came home with a supply of beer and malt liquor, and the empty bottles piled up rapidly. Whereas before he had driven me out of his life physically, now he pushed me out psychologically as well, supplanting me with the false comfort found in bottles and pills. Periodically he got violent and abusive towards me. Whenever I sensed a mean spell coming on, I quickly put the baby in the stroller and escaped with him to the park.

One day, John went completely berserk. He picked up a chair and heaved it against a window. I screamed as glass shards exploded into the room. He had a vacant far-away look in his eyes that frightened me. I watched in horror as another chair went crashing through the window. Next he threw the television out of the back door.

Terrified, I picked up the baby, ran to a neighbor's house and called the police and paramedics to come and restrain John. I knew I had to get away, but where? I had no family in Akron. I decided to hide out at the apartment of a friend named Tommy. He took me in, and I ended up staying with him for the better part of a year.

Chapter 3

I finally had to admit to myself that something was profoundly wrong with Corky. He was too quiet and passive. I sang to him all the nursery rhymes and lullabies I could remember while cradling him in my arms. I talked to him while I changed his diapers. I sang gospel songs to him, and slow ballads I heard on the radio. He was like a lump of clay, or a sack of potatoes in my arms. He never looked directly at me - not a flicker of recognition.

Sometimes I felt like shaking him in my frustration.

"I'm your momma, Corky, and you're my baby boy. Do something, dammit, don't just lie there! What's wrong with you? Look, this is how you smile." I put my fingers at the corners of his mouth and turned them up. When I took my fingers away, his lips fell back into their usual repose.

Toys didn't interest him. I shook rattles at him, dangled beads in front of him, put a fluffy teddy bear in his arms. He never reached for the toy; the teddy bear fell to the floor. When I approached him to pick him up, he never raised his arms, like normal toddlers do.

The hyperactivity started as soon as he could walk.

"Don't scream, Corky, please! You've got no reason to cry or scream. You ate your strained peas and emptied your bottle, and you've got a dry diaper. Now stop running from room to room!"

How could this happen to me? I'd been a good girl, why is God punishing me? I took good care of myself the whole nine months. Why isn't my baby normal?

When reality hit me, I fell into depression. I felt like a yawning abyss had opened under me, and I was falling, falling, into a pit I would never be able to climb out of.

I'd had such plans for Corky. He would finish high school. He would travel with me when he got older, to the cities where I would have dancing jobs. He'd be a good student, maybe a good musician too. He would not, like so many men I knew, succumb to the illusions found in a bottle of malt liquor. He'd find a nice girl, a sweet pretty girl, and learn to make a commitment - not like the men I knew, who continually tried to prove how manly they are by scoring with as many girls as possible.

Would any of this be possible for Corky?

I took him to a doctor to find out what was wrong, but I don't think the doctor could come to a definite conclusion. His diagnosis was hearing loss and brain damage, resulting in retardation.

I couldn't bring myself to accept this. Would my baby be doomed to live in an institution, warehoused away, never to delight in a beautiful sunset, a stirring melody on a violin, a whispered phrase from a loved one? Surely some day, with proper treatment, my son could become normal. I longed for the day when I would hear him say Mama. I yearned for the day when his little round face would break into a smile when I got him up in the morning.

Corky and I took long walks around the neighborhood. He was content to hold my hand as we ambled along over uneven sidewalks. He seemed to enjoy visits to the nearby playground. I pushed him gently on the swing, until my arms got tired. Besides the swing, he also liked the rhythmic motion of the seesaw.

Corky could feed himself at age three, and learned to dress himself soon after that. Learning to brush his teeth was no problem. For discipline, I occasionally spanked him, but I found that screaming at him was more effective. For rewards, I used candy when he was little, and lots of praise. Whatever discipline method I used, it never provoked tears or crying spells.

Toilet training Corky was a nightmare. For at least three months, I kept him in the bathroom much of the time, along with several toys that for the most part remained untouched. I wanted to make the bathroom a fun place to be, not a place of conflict. On some days I even served him lunch in the bathroom. Finally he caught on to what the toilet is there for.

We slept together in the same bed, and I rubbed his back and massaged his little arms and legs endlessly.

Trying to get Corky to talk, I laid him on my stomach, put my mouth close to his, and made noises, like "puh-puh-puh" or "sh-sh-sh". I placed his hands on my throat while I made vowel sounds - "ah-ah-ah, ee-ee-ee" - and then on his own throat. I gave him a harmonica when he was three or four. The idea behind that was to let him find out he could make sounds with his mouth. He enjoyed the harmonica for many years, and got to be quite expert at playing it. As he grew older, he'd run and get the harmonica when a favorite TV show came on, and play along with the show's theme song.

I knew I needed professional help for Corky by the time he was four, so I took him to a neurologist. This doctor gave Corky an electrocardiogram and administered other tests. "Corky is profoundly retarded" was his diagnosis. A cold wind blew inside me when I heard that. My mouth puckered as I tried to hold back the tears fighting their way out. My beautiful son retarded? It couldn't be!

I just couldn't accept this doctor's diagnosis either. I never filled the drug prescriptions he gave me. I was hoping for a magic key that would unlock Corky's mind and allow him to let other people enter. But apparently no such key existed. I couldn't bring myself to dose him with drugs. My patience and endurance were the only factors that might lead Corky into verbal communication.

Most of the time Corky was hyperactive. He would race around the house, never sitting still for more than a few minutes. Often there would be screaming fits for no apparent reason. Sometimes he clapped his hands over his ears, as though the sound was causing him pain. Putting him in a tub of warm water helped to calm him down. Also, I found a motel with a swimming pool where I could swim even though I wasn't a paying guest there. I went mainly because of Corky; he loved splashing and playing in the shallow water.

I enrolled Corky in speech therapy at Akron Children's Hospital, hoping this would elicit some semblance of speech from him. Every week we took a bus and I left him with the speech therapist for an hour. When I returned, it was always the same: the therapist shook her head sadly, meaning No, he didn't utter a word.

For a while I had an old upright piano that Corky liked to bang on. For some people, that kind of noise would be irritating, but I didn't mind it. It was a harmless activity for Corky, as far as I was concerned. Anything that would calm him down for even a short period was okay with me.

I found I could relate to Corky without words. Just like one can tell when a plant needs water, I could tell when Corky needed something by looking into his eyes and listening to his moans. Also, he would point or climb onto the kitchen counter when he wanted something. When he refused something being offered, he shook his head or pushed it away. His mannerisms let me know whether he understood what I said to him. If he calmed down, I knew that he understood me. This proved to me that he had some basic intelligence.

Chapter 4

I realized Corky needed various sorts of therapy, and this would cost money. I had a regular job as a nurse's aide, and evenings I was a go-go girl in a nightclub, dancing to throbbing music in a cage suspended high off the floor. My friend Tommy kept Corky while I was working. He even took Corky along during his shift as a taxi driver.

I enjoyed the dance job more than the nurse's aide job. I felt that I was always meant to be a performer of some sort. That became my desired destiny when I sang "More Than You Know" in my high school talent show. As I finished my song, thunderous applause exploded from all corners of the auditorium. For the first time in my life, I felt that I was really somebody. I floated off-stage feeling that Heaven had finally smiled upon me. This was a reaction I wanted to re-capture as often as possible.

The dance lessons that Mommy enrolled me in as a child taught me the basics of ballet. I had been a lanky uncoordinated little girl, forever dropping things and stumbling over my own feet. Mommy decided that dance lessons would make me more graceful in my movements. At Miss Selfridge's ballet classes I learned to twirl and bend and move my feet elegantly into prescribed positions. Following the directions of Miss Selfridge's pointing finger, I took my turn tiptoeing in dainty small steps the length of the room. With slowly raised arms, we pretended to be blossoms opening in the sun. Flapping arms made us butterflies flitting from flower to flower.

I loved the dance lessons. They made me feel free, and proud of my tall slender body. My dancing lessons progressed to pliés, pirouettes, and arabesques. Then, when I was about nine, I had an unexpected meeting with a professional dancer.

Caldonia was a popular black exotic dancer who was scheduled to appear at the American Legion Hall in Alliance. For days nobody could talk about anything else. Anticipation hung in the air, as palpable as the sweeping wind heralds a coming summer thunderstorm. I listened to the talk and took in all the excitement. I knew it was something children were to have no part in, and this made me all the more curious. Who was this Caldonia person, I wondered. I'd have to find out for myself.

The evening of the performance I crept quietly out of the house and sneaked into the back entrance of the American Legion Hall.

"Lordy, whose child is this?" Caldonia exclaimed when she spied me in the corridor. She was thin and well-built, with high cheekbones and a mass of long silky black hair.

"I wanted to see who you was, 'cos everybody be talkin' 'bout you."

"Well, come on in my dressing room. You want to see the costumes I wear when I dance?"

Her costumes were the most beautiful garments I'd ever seen - like something out of a fairy tale - shiny material covered with sequins, and long filmy scarves. I couldn't stop looking at them. I didn't dare reach out and touch one, afraid it might disintegrate under my fingers, the way a spider's web is destroyed by a probing stick. Finally Caldonia said, "You better go back home now, before your momma whip your butt." She shooed me out of the dressing room. I lingered at the end of the corridor until she emerged to make her stage entrance. I heard the crowd roar as she came onstage. Then, reluctantly, I left. Running home, I had just one thought: Maybe some day I'll do what Caldonia does.

After the stint as a go-go girl, other dance offers followed. I started adding my own moves to the dance routines, to personalize them, just like I used to jazz up the songs my high school music class sang, much to the teacher's consternation. I improvised dance costumes by adding scarves, beads, and sequins from the Goodwill store to swimsuits and skirts.

One of my gigs was at a place called "The Baby Grand", which engaged top entertainers like James Brown, Tina Turner, and Ella Fitzgerald. I talked to Tina Turner once for a couple of minutes during her break, and decided that she's a very nice, down-to-earth person. Year later, I read that she left her husband Ike, accusing him of years of abuse. I felt sorry for her, but without Ike she might not have become a star entertainer; perhaps the abuse was the price she had to pay for stardom.

Besides dancing experience, I also got some lessons in human behavior. A guy I knew named Troy used to pick me up, all decked out in a very short aqua dress with gold sequins under my coat. He'd park near a restaurant that was next door to where my dance gig was.

"I want you to come and walk up and down with me in front of this restaurant," he told me. "You ain't gotta do nothin'. Just open up your coat for a moment whenever I tell you. Each time you do that, I'll give you twenty dollars."

So the two of us paraded from one area illuminated by a streetlight to the next, and back again. Every now and then Troy said "Okay, baby, open your coat up."

I pulled my coat back, just like a flasher, turning my head aside in a regal fashion.

"Okay, button up. Go in the restaurant and have some coffee. I'll be with you in a minute."

I went into the restaurant, and pretty soon Troy came in and slipped me a twenty. By the end of the evening, I found myself richer by about a hundred dollars. This went on for several evenings.

The restaurant was on the street floor of the building. There was a stairway going to the second floor from just inside the front door, and another stairway inside the back door. Both stairways met on the second floor landing. A dim light near the front door barely lit up the stairs.

One time I decided not to go into the restaurant when he told me. I opened the outside door and then loitered at the foot of the stairs to see what would happen. I heard Troy's voice upstairs on the landing:

"Give me your f—money,—or else…"

Then another voice: "Here, that's all I have. Now put the gun away."

The grim realization hit me, like blinders falling off to reveal a glaring reality: He's robbing these men! He's using me as bait to lure guys to come in, and then he's holding them up! So that's where all the twenty dollar bills are coming from!

We were in the red light district of Canton, cars cruised the streets continually, hookers with thick mascara circling their eyes drifted in and out of the restaurant, and here was I, in this milieu, inadvertently flagging down cars for my so-called friend. Every time I opened my coat and then disappeared into the restaurant, he told the eager john, "She's upstairs waitin' for you." The man entered the front door,

Troy ran around to the back, met him on the landing, and relieved him at gunpoint of his money.

I was repelled by what Troy was doing, but I sure could use the money. Just one more night, I told myself. Then the next night again - just one more night.

After a week and a half of this, I decided I wasn't cut out to be a decoy. I told Troy, who was about to become my ex-friend, "I'm quittin' my dance job. My mom is comin' to get me tomorrow. She hasn't seen me in a month, and she's takin' me home."

Disappointment clouded his face.

"Well, if you ever come to Canton again, please call me."

He probably found himself another naïve dancer to be his decoy.

Chapter 5

I desperately wanted a decent male role model for Corky. However, all my perceptions regarding African-American men are filtered through my earlier experiences. That's why I have ambivalent feelings towards them. From time to time I fell in love with one, thinking here is someone I could rely on, but sooner or later the rapport and attraction shriveled and dried up like a fallen leaf in November. Each time it just reinforced my belief that basically African-American men cannot treat a woman with the respect she deserves for any length of time.

My earliest recollection was of my stepfather Roscoe beating my mother in the hilltop house in West Virginia where we lived. He had a steady job in the coal mine, but it was a hard life of poverty for us. When she couldn't take the beatings any more, Mommy packed up her three children and moved us into her mother's house in Alliance, Ohio. Occasionally I overheard Grandma telling Mommy, "That man of yours no good. He don't send no money for your children."

After a time Roscoe followed us to Alliance and was reconciled with my mother. At first I was happy to have him living with us again, but in my pre-teen years those feelings changed.

"Come and give me a massage," Roscoe would say to me. Eager to gain his approval, I ran my fingers over and around whatever body part he indicated. I considered all parts of the body equivalent; to my mind, none had any special significance above the others.

I did this off and on for about a year, until one day I rebelled, and decided I wasn't going to accommodate him any more.

"You ain't gonna do that no more," I yelled. "Don't ask me. Don't come near me!"

I never told my mother, because I thought no one would believe me. Besides, I didn't want to pile more worries on her - she had enough of her own. She loved Roscoe, and I didn't want to come between them. Mommy always tried to give me an extra dose of love, because I was his stepchild, whereas the other two were his own. But I was still the darky, inferior to my light-skinned half-sister.

I'd always been a difficult child to keep in line, but after that I became more unyielding and stubborn and resistant to discipline. The reason, of course, was that I had lost all respect for my stepfather. I didn't want to be home, unless there was no other place to go. I began to spend all my free time at the home of a neighbor woman whom I called Aunt Sarah.

One Friday, the summer I was fourteen, Roscoe came home and confessed he had gambled away his paycheck. There was no money for groceries that week. My mother could have chewed him out, but she didn't. I saw that here was my chance to do something for my family and for my self-esteem.

I waited till dusk, then took several garbage bags from our supply cabinet, and headed for a vegetable garden owned by a woman named Mrs. Pettazzolli. She had about twenty acres at the edge of town where she planted corn, beans, cabbages, zucchini, and tomatoes. In the summer she loaded up her Country Squire station wagon with produce and went door to door to sell it, first in the black community, and if anything was left, then in the white part of town. She looked like a gypsy - a red and green bandanna tied over her black hair, a skirt reaching to her ankles, gold rings on her fingers, and a string of shiny beads around her neck. Deep creases in her leathery cheeks attested to many hours of outdoor labor.

As I hurried down the road, lightning bugs flashed all around me, and mosquitoes whined past my ears like tiny buzz-saws. Overhead, a nighthawk darted this way and that, its hoarse screech cleaving the silence.

The cornstalks loomed ahead, green and dense. The cabbages, ghostly pale in the dying light, were as big as soccer balls. Tomato plants strained to remain erect against the tug of yellow and red spheres. Quickly I filled the plastic bags and returned home, one bulging bag over my shoulder like Santa Claus's pack, and the others dragged behind me.

"You shouldn't have done that!" Mommy said, as I poured an assortment of vegetables onto the kitchen table. "Mrs. Pettazzolli would have let us buy some on credit." But even as she spoke, she began shucking corn. I did feel a little guilty, but after a week of good eating, my guilt subsided.

Up to that time my figure was like the trunk of a tulip tree - tall and straight. By fifteen or sixteen I had leafed out into a mature fullness, like greenery hiding its supporting framework. I was attracting male attention; but mostly it wasn't the right kind.

An older man I knew - he must have been at least 26 - asked me to take a ride with him one evening. "I'll buy you some ice cream," he said. I wasn't very knowledgeable for sixteen, so I got in his car. He drove way out into the country, where houses were far apart.

I started thinking, where is he taking me for ice cream? It must be very special ice cream if he's driving so far to get it.

The houses gave way to cornfields and pasture. The cornstalks were brown and parched after the hot summer. Black-and-white cows eyed us from the fences enclosing their pastures. Finally he turned and parked on a lonely dirt road.

"You are so pretty," he said, pulling me closer. "You about the prettiest girl I know." His hands started roving over my bosom.

"Stop!" I said. "Quit doin' that!"

"Take off your clothes, and you better not tell no one!" His voice had taken on a hard edge, like laser-cut steel. Next thing I knew, cold metal was pressed against my temple. In one quick motion, he had pulled a gun from under the seat. My heart plunged downward like a skydiver without a parachute. But I faced him defiantly.

"Stop it! You keep doin' that, and I'm gonna pray to God every day that somethin' bad will happen to you. I'm gonna go to church every Sunday and pray God will punish you!"

That stopped him cold. He lowered the gun, muttering "Okay", and stowed it under the seat. He drove back into town in silence, dropped me off somewhere in my neighborhood, and I ran all the way home.

Another lesson regarding men came while I worked as an elevator operator at the Sheraton-Mayflower, which was then the most elegant hotel in Akron. Anyone of importance coming to Akron stayed at the Mayflower. Pearl Bailey came one time; she gave the impression of being a happy person, smiling and cracking jokes with everyone. Another time Christine Jorgensen stayed at the hotel; she was known as the first person to undergo a sex change operation, having been born George Jorgensen. I was impressed by the full-length leopard coat and matching shoes that she wore.

I was naïve and celebrity-happy. The hired help were not allowed to be in any rooms with guests. But when one man, part of a visiting basketball team from South Carolina, invited me up for a party, I sneaked back into the hotel after finishing my shift. My heart beating wildly in anticipation - or perhaps because I knew I was not supposed to be there - I ran up the stairway. I knocked hesitantly on the door, and a deep voice called "Come in!" When I entered, I saw the room was empty except for the man who'd invited me. He grabbed me, reached under my skirt, and tore off my panties. I screamed. A security man came running.

"He tore my panties off!" I wailed.

The security man sent me home, minus my panties. I learned my lesson: If you're invited to a party in a hotel room, proceed with caution.

I then enrolled in a clerk-typist course. Two male students came to pick me up each morning for class. One day, as I got in the car, one announced, "We ain't goin' to school today."

"Where we goin'?"

"You'll see."

"One of you guys got a birthday or somethin'? Are we gonna have a party?"

Silence. The driver pulled into Glenwood Cemetery and stopped near a tall monument. It was a cool gray morning. The sun was barely up but invisible behind a bank of pink-streaked clouds.

"Get out and take off your clothes," the guy in the passenger seat said. His voice had a rough, unfriendly tone.

I took a deep breath. "If you harm me, God's gonna git you guys!" I thundered in my best fire-and-brimstone voice. "You'll have to kill me and chop me up into little pieces for me not to get back at you."

They looked at each other questioningly. I could see they were losing their nerve.

"God'll get you if you do anything wrong!" I repeated.

"Okay, okay, we ain't gonna do it."

We drove to school in silence. I never accepted a ride from them again.

Chapter 6

As Corky grew older, he liked jigsaw puzzles - eight to twelve pieces at first, later eighteen to twenty pieces. By age six he got quite good at these, so every Christmas I bought him a new one. Building blocks didn't hold much interest for him. I think the reason was that so much testing at Weaver School involved manipulating blocks. Weaver emphasized developing motor skills and learning to follow commands.

One of Corky's toys that came to be his favorite was something called "See and Say"; when a string on the toy was pulled, it emitted the sounds of various farm animals - moo, baaa, oink, quack, etc. He liked this toy so much that he continued playing with it for many years, well into his teens. Years later, I realized that it gave him satisfaction to be in charge of sounds, and that these sounds were familiar and predictable to him.

I started giving Corky domestic tasks when his screaming or kicking tantrums got to be too much for me. I placed his hand on a cleaning rag with Endust or Liquid Gold on it, put my hand over his, and made rotary motions to polish a table surface. Or I put cleanser on a rag and had him scrub the tub or washbowl. The repetitive motions calmed him, and he was content to keep them up until he was tired. A Brillo pad and a cooking pot could keep him occupied for perhaps a half-hour. "Shiny, shiny" I said to him as the pot took on a gleaming surface. With a spoon, he could bang on the pot also, making what to him was a pleasant ringing sound.

How to behave properly in a store was a difficult thing for Corky to learn. He would see something he wanted, and have a tantrum when told he couldn't have it. We would fight physically, practically rolling on the floor, until he learned to control himself when we were shopping.

Once at the drugstore he showed me a Hershey bar he had picked up. "You put that back," I told him. "We are not buying any candy bars." I took him by the hand and led him to the candy bar display. "Now put it back." He obeyed meekly.

I realized there were similarities between Corky's condition and two individuals I had known earlier. I used to be at Aunt Sarah's house a lot, to get away from my stepfather's demands. She taught me many household tasks - how to wash clothes, how to sew and mend, how to keep a house clean, how to can vegetables, and how to make jelly. But besides these useful skills, I learned how to interact with Todd.

Aunt Sarah's son Todd was a full-grown man, but childlike and very limited in his speech. I helped Aunt Sarah care for him; I read stories to him, walked around the block with him, and played with his toys.

"Let's build a house," I'd say. "See, we put these blocks together, like this. Now you put one on. Good! Now put another one on top."

On our walks, I pointed out items to him. "Look, Todd, look at that tall tree. There's a squirrel climbing up the tree." Or "Look at the leaves on that tree, Todd. See how red they are? Red and orange. That's what happens to leaves in the fall of the year." Sometimes he would look where I pointed, but other times not. He rarely spoke any words.

Later on, another neighbor in Alliance had a daughter named Barbara Jean, a fair-skinned black girl of fourteen with reddish-brown hair done up in braids. Her only words were Huh? and Uh-uh. All day she sat by a window, twisting a little piece of brown paper around and around her fingers. But I found I could relate to her. I played with Barbara Jean's toys and talked to her, whereas her own family largely ignored her. I guess I was the only person who was kind to her.

It was ironic that these early experiences - seeing how these two individuals were rejected by their own families but responded well to companionship and kindness - trained me for the real challenge of my life, a challenge that I couldn't imagine as I came of age and tried to find my place in the world.

It took four years of attending Weaver School before I recognized any improvement in Corky's behavior. He was now almost nine years old. The school had taught him to make eye contact with others. It had also taught him low-impact sports: catching and throwing a ball, kicking and bouncing a brightly-colored beach ball, and the like. But the school had not succeeded in getting him to speak.

About that time, I took Corky to Dr. Unabelle Blackwood, a nutritionist. She was a biochemist with a PhD from the University of Maryland, but her plaid dress, Buster Brown shoes, and West Virginia accent showed she wasn't far removed from her Appalachian roots. Whisps of sandy-colored hair straggled over her ears and forehead. Piercing blue eyes over an eagle nose enhanced a serious demeanor.

Dr. Blackwood taught me that certain food additives affected Corky's behavior. Excess sugar made him hyper, salt made him uncontrollable, and chocolate depressed him, making him quiet and even more withdrawn. Dr. Blackwood prescribed organic food. With charts, she explained each vitamin's effect. I used myself as a guinea pig, taking a vitamin or food additive first to discover what it did to me. Only then, after determining there were no ill effects did I administer the substance to Corky. I tried several "chasers" to make the additives go down easily. I also experimented with other supplements I found in the health food stores - garlic, lecithin, and camomile, among others.

I decided feeding Corky organically grown food was preferable to having him on medication. So from then on, I concentrated on using food items and vitamins to control Corky's behavior. Meals were no problem; he could pack away food like a lumberjack. Chicken and pizza were his favorite foods.

Dr. Blackwood's diagnosis of Corky was autism. That was the first time I ever heard the term. I hurried to the library and checked out every book on autism I could find.

Autism, I learned, is a condition in which the brain does not process the input from the five senses properly. The individual may find certain sounds painful, or else he may seek out rhythmic sounds such as from a washer or dishwasher, which he finds comforting. Some autistic children find any touch on their skin painful; others may deliberately hurt themselves in order to experience sensations of touch. Some children can't stand strong smells, while others seek them out. Some focus on particles of dust and are fascinated by things that normal people can't see. To certain autistics, normal speech sounds like a jumble of unintelligible sounds.

Individuals with autism usually exhibit at least half of the traits shown below. In addition, their abnormal behavior occurs across many different situations and is consistently in appropriate for their age.

So it seems that some autistic children hear, feel, smell, or see too well, and others not well enough. In other words, they are either hyper or hypo. In the first group, the stimulation of one or more of their senses is too much for their system to handle. To protect themselves from this sensory overload, they react with fear and withdrawal. Children in the second group have systems that do not allow enough sensory input to reach the brain. In all cases, children can't make sense of the world and so they engage in bizarre actions to compensate.

Sometimes an autistic individual can overcome his handicap and live some semblance of a normal life. But these cases are as rare as a snowfall in May. More often, the individual is placed in an institution, or lives in a sheltered, supervised home. I was determined not to let that happen to Corky.

I tried fitting Corky's behavior into the various categories I had read about. First I drew up a table of various autistic behaviors and asked myself if Corky exhibited these. Then I arranged the behaviors into hyper or hypo. However, Corky could not be said to be definitely hyper or hypo with regard to touch, sound, or sight. There were too many contradictory behaviors. He did exhibit more hypo behaviors with regard to hearing, and more hyper with regard to touch. The only clear statement I could make was that he was hypo with regard to smell and hyper with regard to taste.

At least my reading gave me an understanding of the reasons for Corky's bizarre actions. And that unconditional love, acceptance, and praise were necessary to penetrate the shell that seemed to envelop him, like a ray of sunshine penetrates the dark, gloomy corners of a cave.

The books related two ways of dealing with autism: medication and behavior modification. I didn't care for the medical treatments; they made a child too much of a robot. The methods of behavior modification I felt were too demeaning, like training a dog or a pet monkey. "Sit up and beg, and you'll get a treat" or "Jump through the hoop and you'll get a treat" - that kind of commanding was for animals, not for children. I never used the words "bad boy" with Corky. I couldn't insult his pride; instead, I appealed to his character. I gave him a hug or kiss, and a piece of fruit when he did something he should. Sometimes my singing to him was his reward. I've always felt that pet training and handicapped training should not be the same.

Intuitively I had done some things right with Corky. The rhythm of walking, and swinging, when he was a toddler; the massaging of his arms and legs, getting him gradually used to being touched, and finally enjoying hugs; singing to him, which he could relate to, instead of conversation; calming him with water play; and letting him watch TV, from which he could learn how people behave, without the emotional load of having someone tell him directly.

Did Corky show any of these symptoms?

	Yes	No	hypo	hyper
Move away from another person's touch	X			X
Bang head against wall or otherwise hurt Himself	X		X	
Stroke himself, or other rhythmic touching	X			X (tactile)
Resist breast feeding		X		
Fight being picked up or embraced	X			X
Enjoy strong smells, go around smelling objects	X		X	
Ignore sounds, give appearance of being deaf	X			X
Body-spinning, any dizzying activity	X		X	
Hit objects to produce a sound		X		
Put hands over ears	X			X
Light sleeper	X			X
Frightened by barking dogs, rain, wind noise		X		
Move toward loud rhythmic noises like appliances	X		X	
Have violent screaming outbursts	X			
Gag over strong tastes		X		
Run tongue over objects		X		
Picky eater	X			X
Eat anything; everything goes into mouth		X		

Rocking, spinning, twirling		X		
Look at particles of lint or dust	X			X
Photographic memory	X			X
Attracted to light source	X		X	
Stare at mirrors or other shiny surfaces	X		X	
Finger twisting and hand play	X		X (visual)	
Repeat whatever is said to him	N/A			
Afraid of heights and speed		x		

Chapter 7

In spite of my good income, the bills kept piling up. I was on my own and had purchased a house, a small bungalow. That meant mortgage payments had to be met.

At the club where I was dancing, I met a black woman with the stage name Liana, who was known as the best exotic dancer in the area. A boyfriend of hers was murdered in a drug dispute, and I offered her a comforting shoulder to cry on while she was grieving. We got to be good friends.

One of the clubs Liana and I danced at was called Stage Door Johnny's. After doing three shows each evening at this Cleveland club, I was usually tired, and eager to get home to Corky. One evening, after the last show, the boss knocked on my dressing room door.

"I want you to meet someone," he said, upon entering.

Behind him was a tall, fleshy, round-faced man of about thirty.

"This is Larry Flynt," he said to me. "Larry, this is Marty."

Larry looked me up and down. "I enjoyed your act. I want you and the other dancer to come down to my office in Columbus for interviews. I'm looking for new girls to feature in my magazine. How's next Thursday?"

I was speechless for a moment. "Thursday's fine," I finally stammered. "I'll be there."

"Good." He turned and was gone, along with the boss.

I sank into a chair. Like many people in my line of work, I knew all about Larry Flynt - how he'd started his magazine HUSTLER as a newsletter among the nightclubs that he owned, how it had caught on like wildfire, selling for $2.25 a copy, and creating for him a publishing empire that netted him millions every year and allowed him to live in a 24-room Tudor mansion in Columbus amid lavish furnishings and expensive art objects. I also knew that HUSTLER was the raunchiest pornography that ever came out of a printing press.

Why would he want me in his magazine? To brag that he was the first publisher to feature a black girl as a centerfold? More to the point, why would I want to be in his magazine?

Liana and I took a Greyhound to Columbus and a cab to the Sheraton Hotel where Flynt had reserved a room for us. The next morning we showed up at his office.

Entering his office suite was like stepping into a "Twilight Zone". In the hallway stood a heavily-armed security guard. The inner office, where we were interviewed one at a time, had beautiful mahogany and rosewood furniture, probably each piece an antique. What ruined the décor, however, were the huge photos of girls on the walls, each one in an obscene pose with her legs wide apart. I could see Larry's wife in an adjoining office, conducting business at a huge desk, with a full-length mink coat hanging on a giant antique coat rack nearby. How can such a sophisticated woman, I thought, be involved with such a perverted man?

I might have considered Flynt's offer if it had been enough to straighten out Corky's and my own life. But $2500 wasn't nearly enough to induce me to expose my muffin to the world.

"I know you're paying some girls twenty-five thousand," I told him.

"No. Twenty-five hundred is all any girl gets. So how about it?"

I was sure he was lying. Was he trying to tell me black girls are worth only one-tenth as much as white girls?

In spite of his repeated offer, I declined. When I came down and told Liana, who was waiting for her own interview, she had a fit.

"That could have been the opportunity of your life!" she shrieked.

She went up to the office and was gone a long time. She never told me what happened at her interview. But I know her photo never appeared in HUSTLER. As for me, I was fired from Stage Door Johnny's soon after our excursion to Columbus. I don't know whether Flynt had a hand in my being fired, or whether the management simply decided my act wasn't raunchy enough.

It was ironic that some time before, I had danced for two months at another club in Akron, which Flynt owned and managed himself. He certainly didn't remember me from that time.

One day Liana said to me, "Marty, I've got bookings to dance in Canada. Would you like to come along as my valet? Take care of my costumes, run errands for me - that kind of thing?"

I knew that Canada was a paradise for black entertainers. I think Canada is even more of a melting pot than the U.S., and Canadians are not at all fussy about the color of their entertainers.

I was living with Carl then - a dark, handsome man with luminous eyes who had been introduced to me at a café where I was having a drink with a girl friend. He had asked me to dance, and I sort of melted into his arms. Before long he moved in with me. His caresses sent tingles up and down my spine, and when he said "I love you, Marty" his voice was like warm fudge sauce. I kept thinking this might be my dream man, the one who's going to take care of me from now on.

I was pleased that Carl accepted Corky. Corky and I were a package deal - if you want me, you've gotta take Corky too. We were like a genuine family. And another plus: having Carl in my home allowed me to expand my dancing career geographically. So with no second thoughts, I jumped at Liana's offer.

She was to be in Canada for six weeks. I knew Carl would take care of Corky during that time. As I got ready for the trip, on impulse I added my own costumes to the items I packed. Subconsciously I was thinking if things don't work out with Liana, maybe I'll get a chance to dance on my own.

In Toronto, we were met by Liana's agent. "I'm just visiting and observing this time," I told him. "Maybe later you can get bookings for me also."

For a week Liana danced at hotels in Toronto. I waited backstage or in her dressing room, helped her with costume changes, brought her coffee or tea with honey. Late at night we would return to our hotel room.

Then, inexplicably, Liana disappeared. For four days I waited at our hotel. No word from Liana. Alarmed, I called the agent; he didn't know where she was either. Then he asked if I wanted a booking of my own. Joyfully I agreed. After all, how long could I remain at the hotel with no money coming in? I congratulated myself for having the foresight to bring my costumes.

My booking was in a small town to the north, at a lovely old hotel where a lot of Germans stayed. The pay was good - $450 a week, of which the agent got $50. I guess my beautiful costumes and graceful dancing charmed the audience. The tips were unbelievable - enough for me to clear seven or eight hundred a week.

I tried to save as much as I could, so that I could send it to Carl for Corky's care. In my hotel room, I lived on cereal, fruit, sardines, and peanut butter. I also took vitamins regularly. Of course I got enough exercise through my dancing.

Liana re-appeared, found where I was, and got angry.

"You took my job! " she fumed. "You should have waited for me at the hotel. That should have been my gig."

However, the money meant more to me than her friendship. I was finally making enough to pay for Corky's needs. And I was definitely launched on my own dancing career.

The agent then booked me into a gig in Toronto, where I made the unbelievable sum of $1200 a week. But the most exciting thing that happened to me while in Canada was my gig in Timmins, Ontario.

I was flown in a small private plane for one day into the mountains to perform for about nine hundred retired miners. Timmins is a copper-mining town north of Sudbury, and remote from civilization. In summer, women and children climb over boulders in search of blueberries that grow profusely in the hollows that are filled with soil. In winter, days are short, a cold, raw wind blows, and wolves can be heard howling in the distance.

A committee of miners was on hand when my plane landed, and they fell over one another in their eagerness to help me with my bags. A limousine transported me to a small hotel, and the men made sure I was comfortable before leaving me to rest up before my performance.

The band that accompanied my dancing was well-versed in my type of music. They included the usual strip music, although mine was a class act, more dignified and refined than a strip act. I wore a gold and white outfit and carried a boa that I twirled and during my act would and unwound around myself. The men cheered and whistled when I made my dramatic entrance. Some in the back stood on chairs to get a better view. After my final number, a hat was passed around for tips. For one day's work, I received $2800! My years at ballet school were paying off admirably.

All this royal treatment and munificent pay was a little heady for a black girl from a poor family in Alliance, Ohio. On the one hand, I felt guilty about leaving Corky. He was my responsibility, no one else's. Carl had treated Corky well, but nevertheless, I felt at fault.

After a couple of months at home with Corky and Carl, Liana's agent called me.

"They want you back in Canada. I've booked you for next month."

"I can't go. Last time I was away for six weeks. I just can't do that again."

"You don't have to stay six weeks this time. But you gotta go. Everybody up there wants to see you again."

There is something addictive about big money made relatively easily. I couldn't resist. I started going to Canada two weeks out of every month. Each time I came home with about $2500 in my pocket. Besides paying for Corky's therapies, it helped make payments on my house and my car.

But each time, Carl was upset about my leaving. I felt torn between the money I was making, which benefited Corky, and being home with him, which benefited him in a different way. Should I further my career, or should I stay home and be a mommy to my son? I wanted to be a professional dancer and be respected as such, not some trashy exotic dancer who lies on the floor and spreads her legs. And only as a professional dancer could I earn the money that I needed for Corky. But all the same, I felt guilty each time I left for Canada, and I couldn't hold back the tears when the plane took off.

I took long walks through the streets of whatever Canadian town I found myself in. I gazed at other people that I passed, wondering if they had serious issues in their lives, as I did. I lay awake at night, thinking about Corky, wondering what he did that day, and whether he missed me. The same thoughts percolated through my mind when I awoke each morning that I was away. The two opposing forces, to stay home or to go earn good money, were tearing me apart. I thought of the heroine in "The Red Shoes", a movie I once saw. Like her, I was torn between the desire to dance and the desire to be with the person I love - in my case, my son.

Carl was a good influence on Corky. He took Corky to the movies. He taught him how to catch a baseball. In many ways he was like a father to Corky. But after a year of my trips to Canada, he'd had enough. He was totally against my dancing career.

Although Carl may have loved me for myself at first, I think later he loved my ability to make big money. But finally, even that wasn't enough to keep us together. He was jealous of the men he was sure I was meeting in Canada.

"You ain't my woman no more!' he screamed after I returned from one of my trips. "You everybody's woman now!" Then he spit in my face. That crushed me, even more than his words.

In addition, it was Liana who hastened our break-up. She was fascinated with Carl, and invited him to spend a night with her in a Cleveland hotel. She also gave him some money. Other trysts between the two followed.

Then Liana started calling me up to say "Carl has nice lips", "Carl has good legs", "Carl has a great butt". Finally I decided I'd had enough. I hitchhiked twenty-five miles to Liana's house, wearing my cowboy boots.

I marched in, fists flying. My right hand met her cheek with a resounding slap, while my left hand grabbed her hair.

"How can you be my friend and take my man and call me every day to remind me what you doin' with him?" I screamed.

I balled my fist and swung at her head. My right boot connected with her shin. She finally went down, sobbing. I looked at her with contempt, then left and hitchhiked home.

I sensed a new power surging in me. For once, I felt I was in control of my life. Back at home, I told Carl he'd have to move. I could no longer tolerate him living in my house. So my five years with this tall handsome man with the satin skin and big eyes came to an end.

Eventually I forgave Liana. I'm not one to hold grudges forever. In spite of everything, to this day I consider her a major friend in my life.

I was still determined to have a dancing career, but without the traveling, which was affecting Corky, making him more withdrawn than ever. I set out to get bookings closer to home.

At that time, both the State Theater in Canton and the Astor Theater in Akron featured live entertainment. The Astor was known to be prejudiced against hiring black girls. But I thought if I could dance there I could live at home and be with Corky. So I approached the manager of the Astor and told him I'd be willing to dance for half the usual pay. He said No. Then I offered to dance for $100 a week, knowing that I would get much more in tips. Again he said No. Then I said I would dance for nothing - I was that desperate.

I didn't have to wait long, for something fantastic happened. The well-known stripper and burlesque queen Blaze Starr was booked into the Astor as a headliner. The management told me I could be a co-featured attraction.

Blaze was a sexy, wild-looking woman, with thick lustrous rusty-red hair and big boobs. Her act had unusual props, like dense clouds of smoke through which she appeared. Off-stage, she was down-to-earth, usually wearing skirts and cashmere sweaters.

She told me of her first meeting with her famous lover Earl Long, the governor of Louisiana, at the Show Bar in New Orleans, where she was a featured performer. She told me about their travels throughout the state when he was campaigning for re-election, of his attempts to give black people more rights over the opposition of the state legislators, of their tranquil times at his "Pea Patch Farm", his forced stay in a mental hospital, and his fatal heart attack shortly after being elected to Congress. It was evident to me that she and the governor really loved each other, though their initial attraction may have had another basis on each side. She was crushed when the Long family would not let her attend his funeral.

In her work, Blaze was a perfectionist. I learned a lot from her during our rehearsals. She would make suggestions in a very gentle way. I knew I had a wonderful act, using all my beautiful costumes that I'd had a seamstress make for me in Canada, but under Blaze's tutelage, my act became even more perfect.

Because my show was so remarkable, the management let me dance for free for twelve weeks. It was an exhausting schedule - four shows a day, seven days a week. I couldn't have kept up that pace indefinitely. But I was happy; my career was gaining momentum.

I had for some time considered going to Las Vegas. If I could make it there, I'd be a top banana as an exotic dancer. I confided my ambition to Blaze.

"Go for it," she said. "If you ever dance at the Palomino Club in Vegas, you won't have any trouble getting bookings anywhere in the country."

Chapter 8

Corky's teacher at Weaver School had shown a special interest in Corky and in me. I confided to her that I wanted to go to Las Vegas to further my career. Like a gift from heaven, she offered to keep Corky while I was away. Of course I offered to pay her for her trouble.

I packed up my costumes, my photos, and tapes, flew to Las Vegas, and checked into the Tropicana Hotel. My goal was to get a booking at the Palomino Club. The Palomino was to exotic dancers what the Met is to a soprano, what Mount Everest is to a mountain climber. I felt I needed that under my belt.

I called the owner of the Palomino and asked him to meet me at my hotel, telling him I was afraid I might not be able to find his club. My ploy worked. When he arrived, I had my costumes laid out on the bed, and my pictures, tapes, and contracts from Canada ready to show him. He proved to be a pleasant, short gentleman with a thatch of white hair. He seemed impressed with my credentials.

"Okay, you're on," he said. "You're hired. We'll feature you next week."

I thanked him, and after he left, I could have floated up to the ceiling! All I could think of was Wow! Gypsy Rose Lee and all the big-time burlesque queens have appeared there, and now I'm getting the chance! I'm definitely going BIG-TIME!

Before my first performance at the Palomino, a swarm of butterflies were jitterbugging in my stomach. I ordered a glass of wine from my dressing room, even though I don't normally drink. After downing half of it, the butterflies calmed down to a stately minuet.

The stage with its spotlights and backdrop was perfect for my kind of act. I had chosen the colors of my spotlights to complement my costumes and skin tones. The music on my tapes included Muskrat Love, I've Got Love On My Mind, After Hours, and some Sarah Vaughn songs. I had the music down pat - every note and every move.

When I finished, I got a standing ovation! What a thrill!

I had been performing at the Palomino about a week when another dancer came to perform. She had red hair, and wore rings with enormous rocks on every finger. When she wasn't onstage, big purple-framed glasses were perched on her nose. She rarely sat still for more than a few minutes at a time, and she usually had a lit cigarette in her hand. For her act she had costumes that must have cost five thousand apiece. I could hear the "ooohs" from the audience whenever she made her stage appearance. She had five complete acts, and did a different one for each show.

It turned out that this woman was a journalist who was moonlighting as a dancer. Between shows, she pounded out stories on the typewriter she kept backstage, using her pen name, Susi Midnite.

After one of my shows, she appeared at my dressing room door, a cigarette, as usual, in her hand.

"I want to talk to you," she said between puffs, leaning against the mirrored dressing table. "You know that I write stories for the Las Vegas Mirror. Well, I want to write you up. You're a hit. I can tell you're going places. All you need is good publicity."

I stared at her. "You're really going to do that?" My eyes lit up like a Christmas tree. "That would be wonderful!"

The following week, I got three-and-a-half columns and my picture in the Mirror. This was more publicity than I had even hoped for. Even though all the facts in the story were not true - Susi had given me a nonexistent agent - my head was in the stratosphere, and my walk was springier for weeks after that. I sent one copy to my mom and one to Carl, with whom I was still communicating, even though he wasn't my boyfriend any more.

After the write-up in the newspaper, hordes of casino owners and agents came up to me to shake my hand. I had the feeling that if any of them did me a favor to further my career, sooner or later I'd have to come across with some favors of my own. One chubby gray-haired man asked me to go to lunch with him.

"You need a manager," he told me. "Why don't you let me handle your career? I can do a lot for you."

I told him I'd have to think about it. Career, my foot! What he really wants, I thought, is a little brown sugar. And of course complete control over my life.

He did introduce me to several casino owners, all of whom said, "We read the article about you. Who is your agent? What? You don't have one? You certainly need an agent or a manager!"

But I didn't want any of them. I had gotten this far without an agent, and I wanted to see if I could go further.

My mentor kept bringing me contracts to sign, and I kept putting him off. Then he asked me, "You need a place to stay? That hotel must be expensive. I have a vacant apartment in a building that I own. I can let you stay there until you find something else - if you decide to stay in Vegas."

So I moved into his vacant furnished apartment. Naturally he then expected from me some private, after-hours entertainment in return. I realized that was the price of climbing the ladder to success. In Vegas, you have to put out to stay put - the white girls as well as the black. Many African-Americans call this arrangement glorified slavery: a rich white man helps a black woman get to the top, and then he feels he owns you and expects you to do whatever he says. However, I didn't want to get trapped in such a situation. That kind of arrangement would have made me very uncomfortable. I waited for an opportunity or an excuse to move out.

As usual, whenever I was away from home, I called about twice a week to make sure Corky was all right. The teacher with whom he was staying assured me that everything was fine.

"I miss you, Corky," I said, when she handed him the receiver. "You be a good boy and do whatever Miss Ward tells you." Of course I didn't expect to hear any response from him. Dear Corky! I wondered, aren't you ever going to start talking? What is it going to take to unlock your mind?

Although I was enjoying myself in Las Vegas, thoughts of Corky kept intruding. What was he doing that minute? Was he eating properly? Did he miss me? During one of these moods I discovered a nudist colony nearby, and decided to visit it. I wanted to lie in the sun, feel the warmth wash all over me until I got drowsy, and forget all my problems for a little while. Perhaps shucking off my clothes would banish temporarily my worries about Corky.

I found a space to stretch out on my towel. The sound of chatter in the hot tub and the clack of the ball at the pingpong table almost lulled me to sleep. But while I was oblivious to my surroundings,

Burlesque & Cabaret

Marty Diamond

"Miss Perfect Equipment"

By Susi Midnite

The Automotive Parts and Accessories Association Show, in Chicago, recently chose Marty Diamond as "Miss Perfect Equipment" of 1978. I can see why! Her equipment is in the form of... Marty is a real 38-24-38. She's 5'1" and weighs 145 lbs. Although she's been stripping for three years, she would never... Her goal is to become a high fashion model for magazines such as Harpers Bazaar, and Vogue.

Marty looks extremely elegant on stage with her long, flowing negligees and graceful moves. Occasionally she'll... come out beating a song or two before going into her regular, still-tease routine. She's studied voice, ballet, and jazz for years and it shows.

Marty has only been in Las Vegas for two weeks and would like to stay longer, but she's already booked for the next few months by her busy agent who keeps her on the move most of the time. She eventually wants to "come back and make Las Vegas her permanent home. Marty told me she would prefer to stay in one town instead of traveling from place to place. She also likes Toronto, Canada and wouldn't mind staying there a while. Her designer, Pearl Montago, lives there and she's plan-

...Raquel Welch would give me one of her peach gowns: Marty is a real... She's constantly gripping and never gets tired of it. Being in a situation such as she is, everything looks good on her. I can understand why she would like to make a living as a high fashion model. (She can have her cake and eat it too).

Although Marty loves Las Vegas' cold climax, I still feel because she's crazy about furs and won't have a chance to wear them as much here as someplace else, glad I get it right, Mar-

I asked Marty what kind of food she likes and turns out that she's a health food nut which is great, but I don't see how she can pass up those goodies called "Junk Food." ... I see a combination of both. ... same food for health and beauty and just plain eats them both. Speaking of... thinking of 4 pieces of cake which I'm going to have as soon as I'm finished with this...

She enjoys outdoor activities and likes to read by taking long walks in a quiet...

Pearl Montago used to be a stripper herself so she knows what the girls like best as far as wardrobe is concerned. Marty's favorite color is "peach." She said "I want...

men who are open to new ideas and it's a must that they be healthy. She says "Healthy means a healthy mind." She likes to have a lot of friends and doesn't want to be tied down to anyone in particular at the moment. She is looking for a particular pet, though. She used to have a English Sheepdog which she loved and another one now to keep her company.

Soon Marty will be on her way again. LA and San Francisco are her first two stops. I know you'll have a successful tour Marty. Come back to Vegas soon!!!

I neglected to mention that Marty has been appearing at the Palomino, but by the time this column comes out, she will already have left. Those of you who didn't get a chance to see her will have to wait till her second time around, which may be in late Autumn. All of us girls are happy to work with her again.

men were ogling me. Apparently they had never seen a black woman naked before. And apparently the women nudists didn't appreciate my presence. The manager came over and told me I'd have to leave; my being there was disturbing the others. Yeah, I thought, I'm the fly in the buttermilk. But it was actually ego-boosting to cause such a sensation in a nudist camp. I always thought that in a nudist colony, people don't pay attention to gender, but here sexual jealousy reared its ugly head.

Of course, while I was in Las Vegas, I exploited every opportunity to boost my career. I met a photographer who told me, "I can get your picture onto a calendar."

So he arranged a photo session for me. I was driven out to a ranch, somewhere in the foothills of the Sierra Nevada Mountains.

"This is where I do a lot of my photographic work," Ray, the photographer, told me. "I'll have one of the men bring the horse out."

He disappeared into one of the barn-like buildings, and a moment later one of the ranch hands came leading out a light brown horse with a white stripe down its nose.

I had never been near a horse before, and didn't know how the horse would react to my presence. Would he be disturbed at the sight of a black woman? Would he bolt? Would he kick?

I followed the two men and the horse out into the field, keeping a safe distance behind them.

Sensing my apprehension, the ranch hand said, "This is a gentle horse. He's used to posing for pictures." He petted the horse on its nose.

The photographer got the horse positioned in a spot where mountains would show in the background of the frame. I was to lean against the horse in a standard "boob pose".

"Okay, I'm ready," he said, after fiddling with the camera.

I took off my blouse and leaned backward against the horse. His hide felt soft and cuddly against my skin. The ranch hand was right - he was a well-behaved horse, and apparently knew how to pose.

Click, click, click went the camera, as Ray changed the angle and distance slightly for each shot. Then we were done.

I was Miss June in the JET magazine of 1979. It was distributed all over the world, with me as the centerfold.

So now I had a newspaper feature and an international publication to add to my resume.

Chapter 9

I'm a trusting soul. I trust people too much. But I also trust that I can wriggle out of bad situations as they present themselves.

I'm also impulsive. It was trust and impulse that led me to the Caribbean island of Barbados.

My career was taking off. I wasn't quite ready to return home yet. It was true that I worried about Corky whenever I was away, but when I was home I had to face his unpredictable behavior and use all my energy to handle him.

One of my new friends in Las Vegas was Jack, who worked the lights for one of the stage shows. He was going to be doing lights for the Academy Awards in Hollywood, and he invited me to go to Los Angeles with him. That gave me a reason to leave Las Vegas.

While I was standing at the Los Angeles airport, debating where I needed to go next, a short, very fat man approached me. He had curly brown hair, bulging cheeks like Fuji apples, and an enormous waistline.

"Do you want to go with me?" he asked. "I'm going to Barbados."

"That must be a pretty place," I responded, sizing him up.

"Oh, yes, very pretty. I own a villa there. My LearJet is waiting out on the runway. Why don't you come along, to keep me company?"

He exuded an aura of wealth, power, and prestige. This should be interesting, I thought. My sense of adventure kicked in. I figured I could outrun anyone with all that excess weight, should that become necessary. I followed him to his private plane. He introduced me to his pilot, and we taxied to the end of the runway. As soon as we were airborne, my new friend Al broke out a bottle of Perrier Jouet champagne.

We drank and giggled through much of the trip. He was an architect from San Francisco, he told me. His biggest worry was his daughter, who, it seemed, had a drug problem. He was lonely and needed to talk, and I found him to be good company. I in turn told him about Corky. I felt an instant warm rapport with him.

39

The plane dropped lower, and with a slight jolt we were on the ground, the engines whining as the pilot braked. When the door opened, I could see we were in a clearing at the end of a long runway.

"The groundskeeper will be along any minute with the car," my companion said.

Moments later, a white sedan emerged from a road that had been hidden among the trees. We were whisked down a dirt road that turned into a palm-lined road and ended in front of a sprawling hacienda with a red-tile roof.

Al ushered me into the house, where a giant cotton boll with pink nose and blue eyes came gliding across the marble floor - Al's angora cat, fat like its master.

I admired the still lifes and delicate Chinese landscapes hanging on the living room walls, the jade figurines gracing the side tables, and an enormous aquarium where small blue and orange tropical fish darted through the water.

Al introduced me to the Chinese housekeeper, a small, self-effacing woman whose command of English seemed to be limited. She showed me the spacious bathroom and the jacuzzi made of green marble with gold fixtures. A button on the jacuzzi wall opened sliding doors that afforded a view of the ocean beyond a broad expanse of white sand.

Al and I and the pilot were served dinner, after which Al said he had to make some phone calls. While he was thus occupied, I went outside to explore the grounds.

The sight of the ocean reminded me of my first time at the seashore. It was when Corky was about two years old, when my friend Tommy had taken us to Florida. I had walked into the surf, holding Corky in my arms. My first sensation was a stinging feeling: I realized I must have nicked my skin when shaving my legs. Corky stared at the waves, seemingly entranced by the stipples of sunlight skipping over them, like diamonds glittering when turned this way and that. I helped him make splashes with his hand. "Salty" I said to him over and over, when the waves splashed his face. I wondered now if he remembered anything of those experiences.

Al's garden held trees resembling giant ferns, plants consisting of spiny-edged spikes, and flowers of various hues - pink, lavender, blue, and orange. I drank in all this beauty, delighting in the colors and aromas of the flowers. This was probably the closest to an island paradise that I would ever have the good fortune to visit, and I wanted to make the most of it. Having at last taken my fill of the magnificent garden, I returned to the villa.

Al was still on the phone. I waited in the living room, and a minute later he came in with his face clouded and his fleshy forehead gathered into a frown.

"Something's come up," he told me. "An emergency involving my daughter. I have to return to San Francisco immediately. Please make yourself at home while I'm gone." He hugged me and handed me a wad of crisp one-hundred dollar bills.

I told him I'd wait three days. If he didn't come back within that time, I would leave.

I woke up next morning thinking of Corky and wishing he was there with me. I felt depressed being surrounded by so much beauty and not sharing it with anyone. As the day progressed, my situation filled me with dismay, and I began to cry. I wanted desperately to talk to someone, so I called my mother. Predictably, she disapproved of what I'd done.

"You're always getting yourself into something," she clucked. "What if you're stuck there and can't ever come back?"

After hanging up the phone, I began to sob more than ever. The Chinese housekeeper hovered over me, offering solace: "Jacuzzi? Hot tub? Cup of tea? Make you feel better!"

I spent my time alternating between the jacuzzi and the beach. I sat on the warm sand and watched the waves roll in, and the little sandpipers skitter in and out of the surf. My despondency left me, and I determined to enjoy my stay as much as possible.

On the third day, the pilot re-appeared and told me to pack up: he would take me back to L.A. that afternoon.

What had impelled me to accept Al's invitation? Maybe I thought he could help my career. Maybe I was in an adventurous mood. Maybe I wanted someone to talk to, just like Al did - someone who might understand my concerns about Corky and my efforts to help him break out of his silence. Maybe I was curious about a foreign country I had hardly ever heard about. It was probably a combination of all these factors. Even though my host deserted me and the trip did nothing for my career, I was not sorry I went.

Several months later, a postcard from Paris arrived at my home, saying "You need to come to Paris and take up where Josephine Baker left off. Yours, Al." That was my last contact with him.

My introduction to California was rather upsetting. I wanted to see the ocean immediately upon arrival. I had seen the Atlantic and now I wanted to see the Pacific. Like the Vikings, or the ancient Phoenicians, oceans have always held a kind of fascination for me. I think I could stand for hours, watching the endless waves, the rolling tides, the foaming whitecaps. I felt a kinship with Columbus and the other explorers, who wanted to know what lay on the other side.

Upon arriving at the beach that day, I found it swarming with policemen. I caught a glimpse of an orange tarp, and I thought maybe they were filming a segment of some police show. But someone watching the scene said there was a dead body under the tarp. I had evidently walked smack into a murder scene. That soured me somewhat on L.A.

Next I took a cab to Frederick's of Hollywood. I wanted a pair of beige satin high heels with feathers across the toes, like I'd seen in the movies.

While in L.A., I decided to try out for the Gong Show. I called for an appointment, and was told to bring a swimsuit. Upon arriving at the studio, a perky young woman checked my name on a list and ushered me into a small dressing room where I was to change into my swimsuit. As I undressed and slipped into my yellow one-piece suit, I had the weird feeling that unseen eyes were ogling me through peepholes in the wall. However, I shook off this feeling when the perky young woman led me to a room with a camera and a long table at which four men were seated.

At a signal, I launched into my audition song "Almost Like Being In Love", which I thought I sang very well. There was no reaction among the men. I never got a call back. But I wasn't sorry.

The high point of my stay in L.A. was seeing the Academy Awards from a backstage vantage point. My friend Jack slipped me in, even though security guards were as abundant as flies in a barnyard. He told me to sit in a corner, keep my mouth shut, and DON'T SPEAK TO ANYONE!

I caught a glimpse of Johnny Carson, and of Raquel Welch in a beautiful blue gown. Various celebrities who were presenters paced back and forth, waiting for their moment in the limelight. Around them swarmed the technicians and stagehands whose job it was to make the whole production proceed smoothly.

After a while I got bored sitting there like a store window manikin. It's against my nature to stay quiet for any length of time. I sneaked out the stage door and took a walk. Outside, I struck up a conversation with a driver who, it turned out, was driving Kojak's limousine. We left to have a cup of coffee together, and then he took me back to my hotel in the limo. We had plenty of time to chat because he knew how long-drawn-out the Academy Award presentations are, and he could easily get back before they were over.

I don't remember who won the Oscars that year (1979). I guess that didn't impress me. As glamorous as the Academy Awards are, to me they weren't as exciting as the Grammy Awards. My next goal would be to attend the Grammys.

Chapter 10

I looked out of the window to check on Corky, who had gone outside to play in our fenced-in back yard. He wasn't there. I looked in the front yard, thinking maybe he went there to play. No sign of him in front. Panic arose in me. I felt like I was caught in a tidal wave of misgiving. Had someone kidnapped my son?

I ran from one neighbor's house to another. No, they hadn't seen Corky. My anxiety grew. My heart palpitated so fast I was sure it would jump right out of my chest.

After two hours of frantic searching up and down the street, I found him at the corner drugstore. He was sitting on the counter, calmly eating a candy bar the clerk had given him.

"We knew he was your son," the pharmacist said. "And we knew he couldn't tell us your phone number. We just had to wait until you came looking for him."

I gave Corky a quick hug. There was no reaction from him.

I had flown home from Los Angeles, determined to spend time with Corky. Each time I left him, and each time I returned, I cried. While I was away, I continually wondered: what's my baby doing? He probably needs me. What did he do at school today? Not that he could tell me, but I wondered about it all the same. Did he have any tantrums? Even though he was calmer since Dr. Blackwood recommended food supplements and certain diet restrictions, there were still occasional tantrums. Did he miss me, or even think of me? As much as I trusted his caretaker, I always felt Mommy-care was the best. Guilt would settle on my shoulders again, like a heavy cloak. Corky needed me; what was I doing here, so far away from him?

I told myself I'm only doing this for the money. And perhaps for professional recognition. Good things were happening to me, and the money I was earning was definitely not available in Akron, Ohio. All that money made up for the depression and guilt that I felt. Yet it was an issue that always pursued me, like a possum continuously pursued by baying hounds.

Besides the money, I was proud of myself. I had gone to Las Vegas without a manager or an agent and had got myself a newspaper write-up and a pin-up publication on my own merit. In the burlesque circuit, which is actually a white woman's profession, I had made my mark. Who could predict how far I might go? I knew I could become a star if I kept at it. An African-American burlesque queen! The vision danced through my head, like the pre-Christmas visions of dolls and bicycles of my childhood.

But could I achieve that and still be a mommy to Corky? That was the question, as ponderous to me as Hamlet's "To be or not to be" was to him.

After my break-up with Carl, I was on my own for a long time, always worried - how was I going to make it. The money I'd earned wouldn't last forever. I started taking gigs again, a stag party here and there - anything to bring money in.

Also, I decided to go domestic. I was a good housekeeper, thanks to Aunt Sarah's training, and I had never been opposed to cleaning rich white people's houses, ironing clothes, babysitting, or the like. Through an ad in the paper, I found a gentleman named Frank, whose mother was sick and couldn't keep house properly for the two of them.

Frank was a skinny peanut of a white man, wearing large horn-rimmed glasses, with dark hair slightly thinning on top. He was a World War II veteran, owned a machine shop, and seemed to have few friends and no hobbies to bring him in contact with others. He was very sweet and considerate toward me; he always had a nice lunch in the fridge for me, and a check ready, to pay me for the hours I spent at his house.

Frank took a liking to Corky, saw the potential in him, and began taking him to public places and events. First it was trips to the park, where Corky could use the sliding boards and swings. Then it was movies and restaurants. In winter they went sledding together. In summer Frank took him to carnivals, street festivals, air shows, and Sea World of Ohio. I felt Frank set a good example for Corky, showing him what a kind, decent, hard-working man was like, in contrast to Corky's dad who was never a real father to him.

A couple of times, Frank asked me to come along to a trade show. At one of these, I saw girls standing at the booths, apparently doing nothing but looking pretty.

"What do you do here all day?" I asked several girls.

"Smile, act friendly, hand out pamphlets, get people to put their names and addresses on a list."

They told me they made five or six hundred dollars for three days of doing that! A light flashed on in my head! Easy money!

I made a connection to do a trade show in Chicago. It was an equipment trade show at McCormick Place, an enormous building on Lake Shore Drive. About 90,000 buyers were expected from all over the world.

Of course I had to ask Frank if I could go.

"Sure," he said. "Corky can stay with me and Mother. You go, and enjoy yourself."

In Chicago I was put up in the Sheraton Hotel, sharing the room with two other girls, both blondes. The name of the company I was representing was Perfect Equipment, and the president of the company decided to designate me Miss Perfect Equipment. I knew that a black girl isn't supposed to say No - but what a title to live up to!

The other girls and I went out shopping for outfits and decided on little black T-strap dresses. So I stood at the booth in a slinky black dress and high heels, with a big white banner across my chest proclaiming me "Miss Perfect Equipment." My being a black girl with a well-endowed figure and that white banner attracted a lot of people to the booth. I guess the company president was pleased.

Now I had some money again, and a nice portfolio. But I decided NO MORE, I'm going to stay home and be a Mommy. I went back to my nurse's aide job, which I'd had when I first started dancing. And I continued to do housekeeping for Frank and his mother.

Then his mother died. Frank asked me to continue coming to clean his house. But show business was too much a part of me. I had to find some other aspect of the entertainment industry, where I could get my foot in the door without the constant traveling.

Chapter 11

For as long as I can remember, I was always writing songs. I wrote down the words, and hummed a matching melody to myself. Then I would sing it to certain selected friends.

My friend Geraldine commended me. "Marty, you can write those wonderful lines down, just like that! That is so beautiful!" She asked me to write a poem for her boyfriend, which I did.

While on a dance job in Columbus, I went into a music store and bought music notation paper. I wanted to try to put my melodies down so that a musician could transform a melody in my mind into live music. At the music store I met a pianist named Jerry and sang some of my songs to him.

"Girl, you can write!" was his admiring comment. We formed a team, collaborating on romantic ballads and bluesy numbers. Our talents meshed perfectly; I would sing and he'd write down the notes. We could toss off songs as readily as Don Rickles tosses off one-liners. One memorable night, we created twenty new songs and put them on cassette tapes. Given a phrase or an idea, I can still make up a passable song in about twenty minutes.

Sometimes current events inspired me to write a song. The assassination of John F. Kennedy affected me so profoundly that I shut myself up in my room, and emerged a short time later with a song extolling the President.

But what good is having hundreds of songs if nobody ever hears them?

After my weeks in Las Vegas and Los Angeles, I began planning how to get my songs to the attention of popular artists. I had business cards printed up that proclaimed in gold print "Marty Diamond, songwriter and songstress." I began to save my money. My goal was to attend the next Grammy awards.

Frank graciously agreed to keep Corky again for a few days. I flew to Los Angeles in February of 1980 and rented a limousine at the airport to take me to the Bonaventure Hotel, where I had reserved a room. That was where many of the events would take place, and where all the stars would stay.

I swept into the hotel lobby, wearing a full-length silver fox coat. I felt I was at least an incipient celebrity, and I wanted to look the part, just in case a photographer from the National Enquirer should pop out from behind a column.

My hotel room contained a bouquet of roses and a bottle of champagne, just like I had asked for. I knew I was going to have a good time.

One of the first things I did was head for the hotel boutique. There I purchased a pair of red suede shoes with roses on the toes, and a matching purse. I wandered around the hotel lobby, watching various stars of television and the pop music field check in. I found out that B. B. King, the blues singer, had the room on one side of mine, and Papa Staples of the R & B group The Staples Singers was on the other side. Both were artists I admired greatly.

Catching up with Papa Staples in the corridor, I told him I needed a tag or badge to get into the various events.

"Oh, don't worry, girl, I'll get you one." He kept his promise.

Cindi Lauper shared the elevator with me going up. She had wild orange hair that stuck out at odd angles, and wore bright clothing that seemed mismatched. She acted rather giggly, and I figured she had had a few drinks already. She might have been high on other mood-enhancing stuff. We didn't speak.

It seemed as though the Grammy events consisted mainly of non-stop parties. There was an R & B hospitality lounge, a country-western hospitality lounge, a gospel hospitality lounge, etc. - all stocked with lots of liquor and large platters of food. I stopped in at several of these. In one, I talked to Kim Fields from TV's "Facts of Life" for a few minutes, and slipped her a tape of my songs. I also found an occasion to speak to Roger Miller, who made the song "God Don't Make Little Green Apples" popular.

I wore a silver dress and silver shoes to the main banquet. I was sure I would stand out in my high heels, which made me six foot three. A couple of tables away was Stevie Wonder; seeing him affected me more than all the other stars - he had such a karma and a glow about him. Later I handed Stevie's brother a copy of one of my songs, tied up with a red ribbon, like some sort of award.

On the third and last day of the Grammy events, I was up early in the morning, took the elevator to the top floor where all the suites were, and pushed my business card under every door. The only response I got was from the manager of Andrae Crouch, the gospel singer, with whom I corresponded for a while afterward.

Even though attending the Grammy awards didn't do anything for my career, I'm glad I went. I knew already that you have to spend money to make money. What I learned there was that you just can't meet a star casually and get your music recognized. You have to get to know the managers and agents and theatrical attorneys. But at least I had a wonderful time, rubbing shoulders with celebrities and semi-celebrities.

Chapter 12

I was at long last gaining some measure of clearmindedness where Corky was concerned. For a number of years I'd had to cope with a child that seemed stuck in the "terrible twos" phase. Not much help was available to parents of autistic children then. Drugs were the usual method of treatment, and I rejected that.

Corky became a salt junkie at age nine or ten. For some strange quirk in his make-up, he liked to lick salt, like the deer in the state parks. I often found the salt container from my kitchen shelf in his room. He became hyper and uncontrollable after indulging in this yen, and I had to spank him to get my point across.

"This is bad for you," I scolded. "Come in the bathroom with me." I then poured the salt down the toilet while he watched.

As with other autistic children, incidents that would worry or frighten a normal child didn't faze Corky. Once, while attending a show at the Cleveland Convention Center with Frank and a cousin, Corky got separated from the others in the crowded building. Frank notified the security people, and for a half-hour they and several spectators searched for Corky. When they finally found him, he wasn't the least bit concerned. It was a good thing I wasn't there; I would have been hysterical.

Corky progressed nicely under Frank's influence. His hyper-activity had lessened, and he had no more screaming fits. I felt it was beneficial that he was getting attention from a male role model. Frank was always around, almost like one of the family, sticking to us like glue. But this skinny white man who looked like Barney Fife couldn't possibly be taken for my boyfriend.

Frank started asking me out to dinner, and I went out with him fairly regularly. But I knew I could be nothing more than a good friend to him. One day when I came home, Frank was there waiting for me. He greeted me with a mischievous smile playing around his lips.

"There's a surprise coming later today," he said, watching me closely for my reaction. He already knew that I love surprises.

"A surprise for me?"

"Well, mostly for you."

I was mystified. What could it be? I didn't have to wait long. A pickup truck pulled into the drive. In the back were a shiny new washer and dryer.

I watched, wide-eyed, as the men took out my old washer and dryer and connected the new ones. I felt like I had been transported back to certain Christmases of my childhood, when I had been presented with a long-desired game. My delight was mixed with gratitude toward Frank.

"Thank you, thank you," I told him after the men left. I gave him a hug and dropped a quick kiss on his forehead.

Then Frank took it upon himself to pay off the rest of my mortgage - almost four thousand dollars. More surprises followed. The next big one was a new car - a second-hand brown and white Duster, to replace my old rusted Impala. By this time, my delight was mixed with misgivings. I thought, Oh, my God, where is this going? What is this leading to? This can't go on! Does he feel he has to do this to be part of our lives?

I called my mom and told her of my predicament. She said, "That white man loves you. I don't know what you gonna do." So, as usual, I was back on my own resources. What should I do? That was my first thought in the morning, and my last before drifting off to sleep.

Corky was so happy with Frank, feeling so secure. I guess I really needed Frank around for Corky's sake. But I was confused and baffled. I didn't love him, I was sure of that. I kept thinking, I'm supposed to have a black boyfriend, not a white one. I hadn't had any boyfriend for so long, not since Carl and I broke up. And here was Frank, who had been so kind to us and doing so many wonderful things for Corky and me.

But the most wonderful thing concerning Corky was yet to come.

Corky still was not talking, just sort of mumbling to himself. When he wanted something, he took my hand and led me to what he wanted, or he would point. He communicated by humming - a high-pitched eeeee for pain or discomfort, a lower tone for Yes and a still lower one for No. At eight or nine he could produce a single syllable that would stand for a complete word, as for example ba for banana. For a long time I would finish pronouncing the word for him, as he seemed to expect me to do. Then I decided it was wrong to help him in this way; he should make an effort to say the whole word himself. I still squeezed his lips together to elicit certain sounds, put my lips against his, and had him feel the vibrations in my throat as I sounded out vowels.

I often thought of poor Barbara Jean, the girl sitting by a window, twisting bits of brown paper around and around her fingers, unable to communicate beyond Huh and Uh-uh. Would my Corky end up like that? Not if I could help it! I had a deep faith that something inside him would lead him to respond to the world around him eventually.

One day I was at my kitchen table, going over my bills. Corky, just turned twelve, wandered over, looked at the bills and envelopes spread out in front of me, and pointed to an envelope with the word Plaza on it.

"Pizza," he said, very distinctly.

My heart did a high-jump in my chest.

"What did you say, boy? Say it again!"

I couldn't believe what I'd heard. Plaza wasn't exactly pizza, but that didn't matter. Close enough. Corky had spoken his first complete word!

In a state of joyful shock, I ran to the phone and ordered a pizza to be delivered. With tears and laughter, I fed him the pizza and made him say the word after every bite.

That was the day I became convinced there was hope for Corky. Perhaps my prayers were being answered, finally. Perhaps Corky would now be able to open up and communicate with those around him.

Soon Corky was uttering other words: Yes, no, chicken, bread, eat. I hugged him every time he spoke, and redoubled my efforts with him.

"What is this?" I asked him, pointing at various items of furniture in the house. "Can you say chair? Can you say table?" From then on, I made him say the word for any food item before he was allowed to have it. Also I made pacts with him, like "If you pick up all your toys, you may have some pizza."

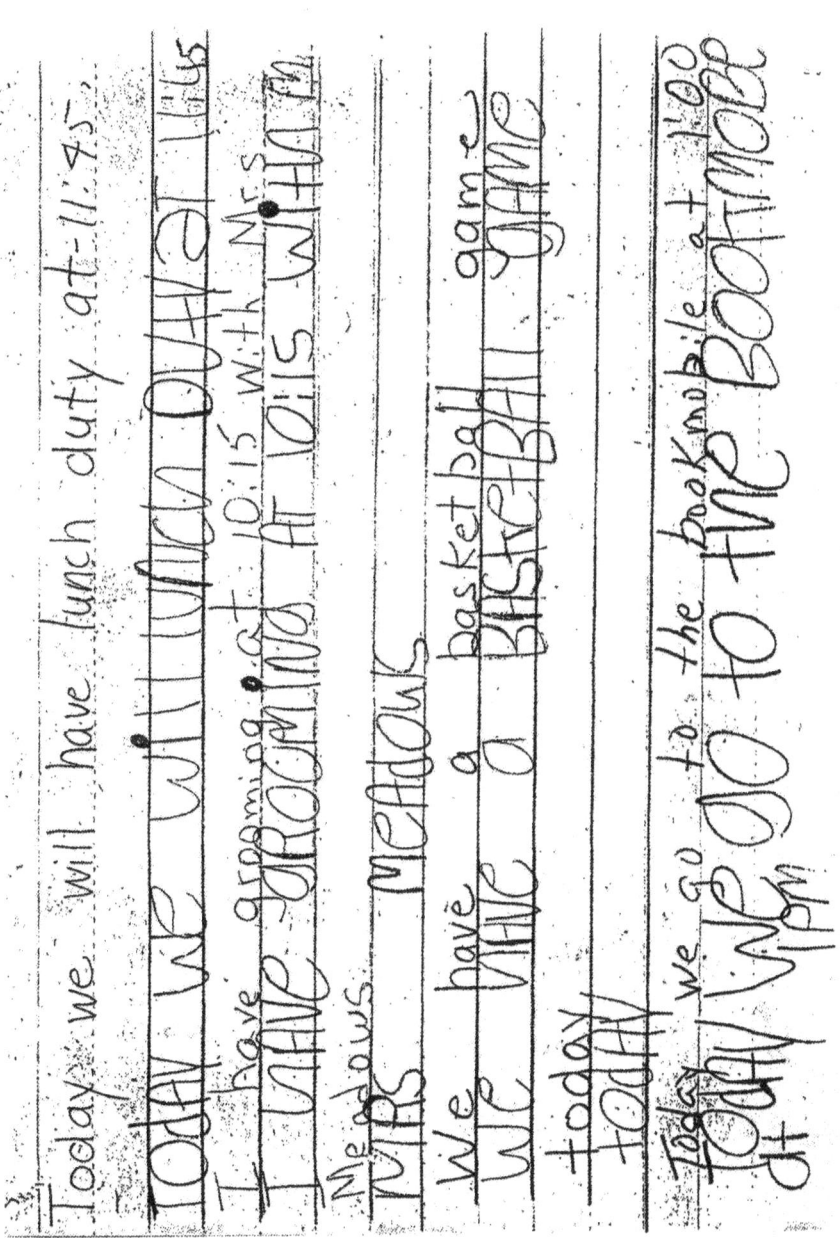

Today we will have lunch duty at 11:45.

Today we will have Duffel Bags

I have grooming at 10:15 with Mrs

I have grooming at this with Mrs

Meadows Meadows

Mrs Meadows

We have a basketball game

We have a Basketball game

Today Today

Today we go to the bookmobile at 1:00

Today we go to the Bookmobile at 1:00

53

Today we will make hearts

TODAY We will make hearts

We will go to the movies at 1:30

WE WILL GO TO THE MOVIES AT 1:30PM

We will go to the bookmobile at 1:00PM

Today is Thursday February 2 1984 I have grooming

TODAY IS THURSDAY FEBRUARY 2 1984 GROOMING

We go to the movies at 1:30

WE GO to the movies at 1:30PM

We will go to the bookmobile at 1:00

WE WILL GO to the BOOKMOBILE at

Today we will have language at 11:00

TODAY We will HAVE LANGUAGE at 11AM

Corky's school papers at age twelve. These
are about second grade level work

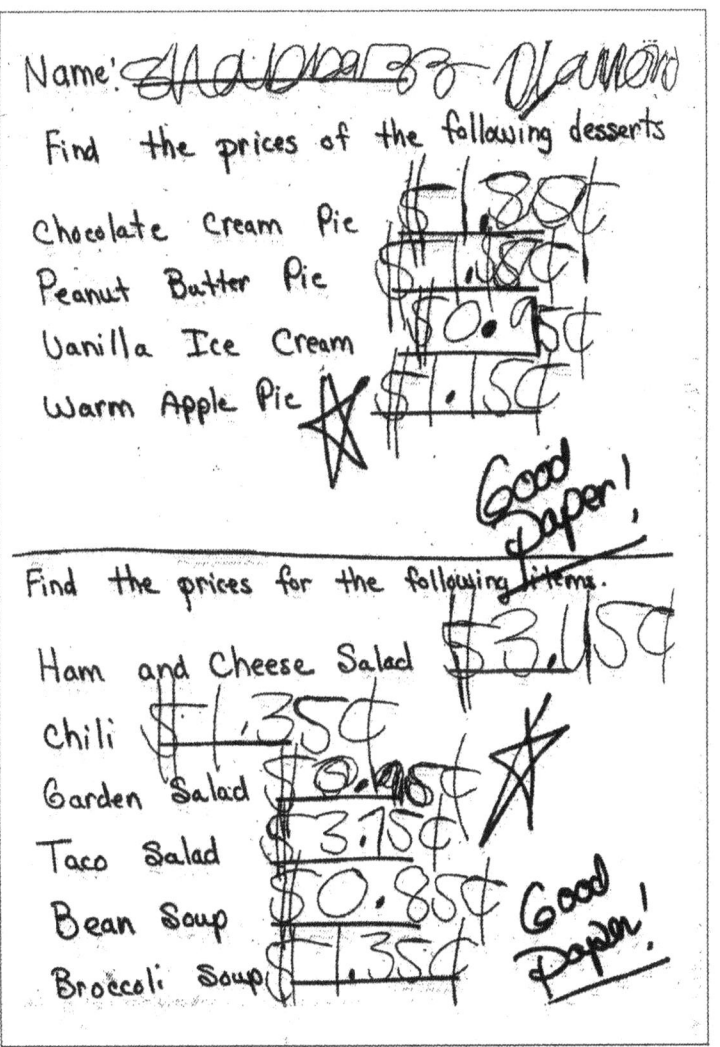

Name: ~~Shadowfox~~ Vamon

Find the prices of the following desserts

Chocolate Cream Pie $1.85¢
Peanut Butter Pie $1.85¢
Vanilla Ice Cream $0.95¢
Warm Apple Pie   ⭐ $1.15¢

Good Paper!

Find the prices for the following items.

Ham and Cheese Salad $3.15¢
Chili $1.35¢
Garden Salad $0.45¢ ⭐
Taco Salad $3.15¢
Bean Soup $0.85¢   *Good Paper!*
Broccoli Soup $1.35¢

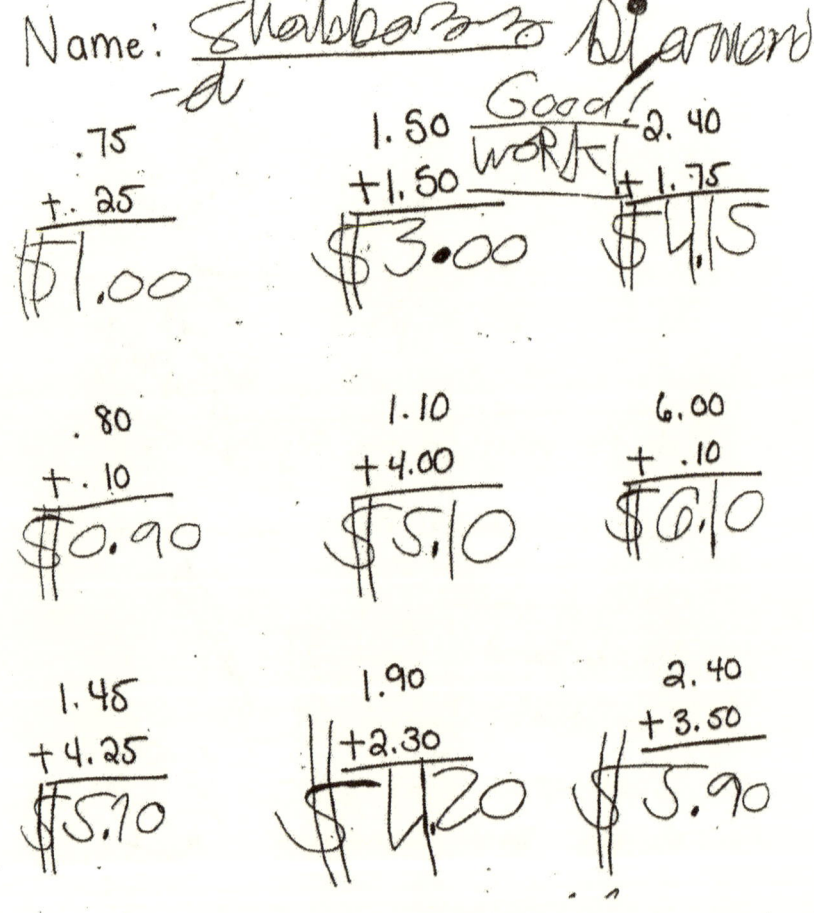

At last, I thought, Corky and I would be able to have conversations. I would get to know him as a person, not as a whirlwind scampering from room to room, or a withdrawn Buddha-like figure, or a screaming, kicking, inconsolable child. John Locke, the seventeenth century philosopher, regarded children at birth as a blank slate on which experiences and sensations are marked to give them a personality. So far Corky had remained pretty much a blank slate, at least judging from his reactions. Now that he found the ability, or courage, or whatever it was that had held him back, to talk, I knew he was not retarded, despite what the doctors had told me. I derived great comfort from that thought.

Corky then started reading street signs, always spelling out the word before pronouncing it: S T O P, stop; N O P A R K I N G, no parking; E X I T, exit. He continued doing this for two years. It proved to me that Corky had basic intelligence. It showed that he could read long before he could talk. This to me was a revelation - that he could suddenly read without specific instruction. He must have absorbed the sounds made by each letter and subconsciously learned to put the sounds together in his head, thus learning to read silently. Or was it watching TV commercials that enabled him to read? Whatever the means, this was a watershed in our lives.

Once I knew he could read, I posted signs all over the house: "Make bed", "wash hands", and so forth. I copied school papers he brought home, made some revisions, and let him work on my versions of those worksheets. I think that reinforced whatever little academic learning he was getting at Weaver School. Weaver gave him structure, a peer group, proper behavior, but I was worried that he was not gaining a true education. Therefore I felt I had to supplement his learning.

Although Corky now knew and could say the names of many things, he still did not string words together. He continued to spell out signs he saw along the streets, and words he saw on the TV screen. Occasionally he said "Eat what?", meaning "What are we having for dinner (lunch)?"

Pronouns were always troublesome. Like most autistics, he didn't understand the difference between I and You, mine and yours. It was another two or three years before he started putting words together into rudimentary sentences. But even then a statement from him might come out as "Mommy eat Mommy's cooking" rather than "I'm going to eat Mommy's cooking." I'm sure he understood the meanings of many adjectives such as good, bad, fast, slow, but there was no way he could let me know that he understood.

I began teaching Corky household chores, even though this took all the patience I had. I stood over him, holding his hand, practically crawling on top of him, to guide his motions. We went through the same motions twenty-five times, whether it was mopping the floor, cleaning the toilet, or scrubbing a cooking pot. I felt it was important for him to learn to do this, for three reasons: it would give him self-assurance and pride in a job well-done; secondly, autistic individuals enjoy doing repetitive motions, and scrubbing was more productive than rocking or spinning objects; and furthermore, it might become necessary in the future for him to know and carry out household skills.

Sometimes Corky resented my persistence. At times he got frustrated and showed it by shaking both hands violently or bobbing his body back and forth like a worshipper in a trance. When I felt he had mastered a job, I let him do it alone, but often the results were unsatisfactory.

"Go back and do it again," I told him after he showed me a pot he had scrubbed. "You didn't get it clean." Sometimes I made him wash the same pot eight times, until he got it past my Sherlock Holmesian inspection.

I bought Corky a saxophone, a used Conn alto sax, and let him fool around with it. I had tried formal lessons on the guitar several years before, but that was useless; Corky just didn't have the attention span to benefit. On the saxophone, he would blow, blow, blow, and enjoy the sounds that came out. Once in a while a semblance of a tune would emerge. Even today he still likes to blow on his sax.

I also acquired an old typewriter for Corky. He got to be a rapid two-finger typist. Mostly he reproduced commercials he had heard on TV and memorized. Sometimes he typed out the names of his classmates at Weaver School, or short messages like "Want to eat" or "chicken". Other times he punched out lines of dialogue he remembered from the movie "Star Wars." Later into his teens, he typed out names he had seen while watching the credits roll at the end of a TV movie. That was how I found out he had a photographic memory. His spelling was marred by typos, but I always felt he knew the correct spellings. Typing out original thoughts was still beyond him.

At times during his early teens, Corky would wet the bed. To help him overcome this problem without making a big issue of it or shaming him, we made up a little jingle that went "Too much juice makes you peepee in the bed, peepee in the bed, peepee in the bed." We sang this together in the evening, and in time it eliminated the problem.

MAUDE WAS RECORDED ON TTAPE BEFORE A LIVE
AUDINCE

DACCE FEVER WAS RECORED DANCE FEVER WAS
RECORDED

BEFORE ANUDINCE THAT WAS A LIVE THE JEFFERSONS
WAS

RECODED ON TAPE BEFORE A STUIDO ANUDINCE MAUDE
WAS

RECORDED ON TAPE BEFORE STUIO ANUDINCE GOOD
TIMES IS

VIDEO TAPE IN FROUT OF THE STUDIO ANUDINCE GOOD
TIMES W

WAS RECORED ON TAPE BEFORE A LIVE AUDINCE DANCE
FEVER

IS VIDEO TAPE IS FROUT OF THE AUDINCE THAT WAS A
LIVE

Example of Corky's typing. He sometimes misplaced letters; the
word 'audience' seemed to have given him trouble.

APPLE A BOY B CATC DOG D EGG E FISH F GIRL G HOUSE H ICE

CAREAM I JAM J KITE K LION L MOON M NEST N ORGANGE

O PIG P QUEEN Q RABBIT R SUN S TARIN T UMBERLLA

VONLIN V WATCH W XRAY X YARN Y ZERBA Z

I think Corky used the dictionary to come up with this list of words.

I got Corky a set of rollerskates and occasionally took him across the street to a church parking lot to let him rollerskate there. He enjoyed doing that, and it controlled his hyperactivity. He also learned to ride a bike that I had borrowed, but that didn't excite him. On the other hand, he became fond of horseback riding, which we did a number of times when visiting my mother in Alliance. We were each helped onto our mounts, Corky on a beautiful chestnut mare, and I on a darker brown one. Our horses paced leisurely in single file along a trail running more or less parallel to a placid stream. They were of course trained to follow the lead horse ridden by an "urban cowboy." I rode ahead of Corky so that I was always within his sight. Every now and then I twisted around in the saddle to look at him and give him words of encouragement. He sat regally straight, like a general leading his troops. "I'm doin' it, Momma, I'm doin' it!" he exclaimed over and over.

Corky started roaming the streets of our Akron neighborhood alone in his early teens. Most often he stopped in the corner drugstore, where the clerks became accustomed to seeing the handsome black boy who never spoke. Later, when he had learned the names of the clerks, he would enter and sing out "Hi Tony! Hi Shirley! Hi Mary!"

In his middle teens, he could make simple purchases: a tube of toothpaste or a bottle of pop. His choice of the latter was made according to a rule apparent only to him: if he was wearing an orange shirt, it was orange pop; if a red shirt, it was cranapple; if a green shirt, limeade, and so on. When he had money of his own, he preferred coins to bills, and so at the drugstore he'd change a ten-dollar bill for a roll of quarters, or other coins that caught his fancy. In his room, he sifted the quarters from hand to hand, spun them, or let them roll on their edge. This, I knew, is a common activity among autistics. Sometimes he stacked quarters or nickels on the floor of his room, watched the pile topple, and stacked them up again, over and over.

Bills held a different fascination for him. He examined twenty-dollar bills closely to find the letter on them that indicates at which Federal Reserve Bank they originated. He learned what each letter stands for - something most people don't know.

Because of his cruising around the neighborhood streets, some of which were heavily traveled, I knew I had to teach Corky how to cross a street safely. This was a task that was to try my patience sorely.

"Look at the traffic light, Corky," I repeated over and over as we came to an intersection. "What color is it? Red. What does red mean? It means Stop. Now the light is green. Green means we can cross."

I made him repeat "Red - stop, green - go" until it became our mantra.

The next step was crossing a street where there was no traffic light. "Look to the right, look to the left, if no car comes you can cross" became our next slogan, to be chanted at every cross street. "What do you do when you come to a street and you want to get to the other side?" I asked him repeatedly, until I thought he had the answer down pat. All the same, I couldn't help but worry whenever I knew he was out somewhere in the neighborhood.

At thirteen or fourteen, Corky's emotions seemed to develop, and he improved in expressing himself. Whereas he used to be aloof and unaffectionate, now he would put his arms around me. Up to that time, he was aware that I was away a good deal, but according to Frank, he never gave any indication that he actually missed me.

Chapter 13

Having Frank at my house or having him take Corky somewhere allowed me to have more of a social life again. I could go out with this or that girl friend and enjoy myself.

One night I was at a bar with a girl friend and I met a fellow named Marlon. He had big soulful eyes that seemed to take in everything at a glance. He took a liking to me, and so we began dating secretly, taking in movies or going to steak houses. I still maintained a decent relationship with Frank, but now I was torn between the two. Marlon knew about Frank, but Frank didn't know about Marlon.

I was in my kitchen one evening when Marlon appeared at my back door. As soon as I opened the door I could see he was in a belligerent mood. He grabbed my arm and dragged me outside to the driveway. I couldn't dodge his blows. He held me with one hand while his fist came crashing into face time after time. I fell, tried to get up, and his fist leveled me again.

"You get rid of that white man!" he shouted. "I can be Corky's daddy! You don't need no white man to be his daddy!"

Corky had come out of the house.

"You hurt my mommy," he whimpered several times. Of course the scene was upsetting to him.

"Go back inside," I shouted between cuffs.

I kept trying to get up, and Marlon's pounding kept knocking me down. I could taste blood, and realized it was coming from my nose. The concrete driveway rose and crashed into my head time and again. He finally let me go and disappeared. I went in and called the cops. My face was dripping blood like a leaky faucet, all over my clothes and the floor, and I could barely see out of one eye.

The police took down a report but could do nothing unless I filed a complaint. I knew they did not concern themselves too much about "black on black" crime. I then called the paramedics, who took me in an ambulance to the closest emergency room. X-rays were taken, but I wouldn't let the hospital keep me there; I wanted to get home.

Part of being a black woman is getting her ass kicked once in a while. It just happened to be my time.

Frank would never beat me, I knew. But here was a black man I had been dating for only six months, and he was punishing me because I had a white man being kind to me and my son. Was it always going to be this way? Were black men always going to penalize me for having a white male friend? Must I forget about ever having a black boyfriend?

Frank saw my face the next day and knew instantly what had happened. We didn't talk about it. All I said was, "I've been punished for having you in my life." We let it go at that.

I had long felt uncomfortable about letting Frank pay off my house. So I went to the realtor and told him, "Please put Frank's name on the deed. That way everything will be fair."

The realtor did as I asked. But there were unexpected consequences. Frank sold his big house and moved in with me.

"Too many memories of my parents in that house," he told me. "And with me here, nobody's ever going to hurt you again."

That part was okay with me, but I realized, Oh boy, I'm really stuck with him now. Up to that time, I'd been happy to go visit him at his house. Having him at my place was going to have an effect on my family and friends.

It proved to be true. My friends felt uncomfortable visiting me with Frank there. But what could I tell him? He was saving me money, and he was wonderful with Corky, who was now talking in a limited way.

I started going back to Canada just to get a break and think things over. One time, I stayed for six weeks in the mountains of Beaverton, Ontario, meditating, trying to decide: Should I stay with this white man or try to break off the relationship?

In one way, I reveled in my separation from Corky, puffed up like a pouter pigeon with the knowledge that I was bringing home each time maybe not quite a king's ransom, but at least a knight's - money that was always allocated to Corky's needs. Our separation gave me a moratorium, a chance to catch my breath and store up a plethora of patience and persistence, which would gradually unravel, like the torn sleeve of a sweater, upon my return. On the other hand, my periods at home were devoted to teaching Corky new skills and giving him all the love and attention I could muster.

I met a black man in Canada, and fell in love with him, even though I knew the whole time I had to eventually come back home to my son. It was a tempting idea to stay in Canada and let Frank keep Corky. But the guilt came back. My problem had me pinned, like a butterfly mounted in a display case. I realized I had to go home and be with my punkin, and make up for Mommy-time I had missed. The money I made in Canada was never enough anyway, I told myself. I had set up a trust fund for Corky. Any additional money I earned just wasn't worth the price of leaving him for long periods. Besides, when he was thirteen, I took Corky to a psychiatrist to have him certified as being autistic. That document helped me get extra income from the government.

After my stay in Canada, I began dancing in Columbus, a two-hour drive from Akron. I maintained two homes, driving back and forth between them, for the next five years. In Columbus I had dance jobs and fixed sandwiches for Joe, the maintenance man in my apartment building. In Akron I had Corky and Frank, cooked chicken dinners, and brewed camomile tea for Corky.

I always burned up the highway to get back to Akron. In order to keep myself alert, I got a CB radio on which I conversed with truckers on the road.

"Brown Sugar, Brown Sugar, heading north," I'd announce myself.

"Hey there, Brown Sugar, I'd sure like to meet you," one voice said.

"I'll make it worth your while to stop at the next town," said another. "How's about meeting at the Mansfield-Bellville exit?"

Other propositions came as fast as Michael Jordan sinking baskets, but I always ignored them. Sometimes I sang songs to the truckers to keep them and myself awake. I kept a clipboard in the car beside me, so that while I drove I could write down new song lyrics as they came to me.

"Let me try this new song on you," I announced to the truckers, and then proceeded to sing to them. Sometimes I got admiring comments, sometimes silence. One of their favorites began "She's a Million-Dollar Baby With a Two-Cent Head."

Sometimes Corky took a Greyhound bus to Columbus to spend a weekend with me. Frank would take him to the Akron terminal and made sure that he got on the right bus. At the other end, I waited for him, always happy and thankful that he was safe. I'm sure he felt proud to be traveling alone. For him it was a tremendous accomplishment. The Greyhound drivers got to know him, and greeted him cheerfully: "Hi, how are you today? Goin' to Columbus again? Gonna see your momma?"

"Gonna see Momma," Corky responded, emphasizing each word. Conversation to him most often meant repeating the last thing that was said to him.

On one of these visits, I introduced Corky to Paul, a young man I had become friends with, who did odd jobs like painting and carpentry. Paul was a LeVar Burton look-alike, well-built and powerful, but he had never learned to read or write. I had told him so much about Corky that he was eager to meet him.

Paul took Corky frequently to the basketball courts near my apartment building. Corky, who was now reading on an elementary level, spelled out the street signs they passed on their walks, just like he did at home. "S T O P, stop; E X I T, exit; R I G H T right T U R N turn O N L Y only." Soon Paul was reading the street signs too.

One afternoon, as the two of them walked together near my apartment, some young punks approached them.

"Hey, give me that cowboy hat," one said menacingly, eyeing Corky's leather headgear. The two continued walking in silence. "I said give me that cowboy hat," the boy repeated.

"Let's get back to the apartment," Paul said in a low voice. "I'll take care of them later."

They quickened their steps and entered my apartment. Paul swung a baseball bat onto his shoulder and went to face Corky's tormenters. The punks were hanging out in the alley behind the building. Paul came at them, swinging the bat like a Japanese Kendo master brandishing his staff. The punks scattered. Paul was not about to let anybody bother his friend Corky, who had taught him to read and to whom he was forever grateful. Paul was Corky's first true friend. That friendship was an important step in developing his social skills.

Chapter 14

Corky sat beside me in a blue and white motorboat on the Ohio River, each of us with a fishing line plumbing the depths. Mist still hovered over the water this June morning, veiling the trees on the far shore. In the eastern sky, the sun played peek-a-boo among the fluffy clouds. Bird-songs sounded from the shore, which Corky tried to imitate. Swallows played connect-the-dots over our heads, and a heron stood guard in the shallows. The river moved sluggishly where we had dropped anchor, and the current rocked our boat gently like a giant cradle.

Suddenly Corky's mouth flew open and his hands began to shake violently - signs of great excitement.

"You've got a bite!" I said. "Reel it in quickly, like I showed you." A moment later, a beautiful bass flopped on the floor of the boat.

"Look what you caught! A bass! Congratulations, Corky!" I took one hand off my rod to shake his. "Now put him in the bucket. He'll make a good dinner for us tonight."

We had, for the whole summer, the use of a trailer and a boat that belonged to Joe, the maintenance man in Columbus. We fished almost every day, catching bass, walleye, and catfish. It was a wonderful time for both of us. The one-on-one constant interaction with Corky led him to communicate more than ever. It gave me the opportunity to teach him how to prepare healthful meals. He became adept at chopping the heads, tails, and fins off the fish we caught, and frying them.

We cut food pictures out of magazines, and I had Corky arrange them into menus for various meals in order to teach him nutrition.

"Here's a picture of a cheese sandwich. Is that good for you? Would you eat it for breakfast, lunch, or dinner?"

"Lunch," he'd say, bobbing his head for emphasis.

As a teen, Corky had begun puttering around in the kitchen, and I realized I had to teach him the hazards of kitchen work, as he still had no concept of dangerous situations. I took his hand and passed it over a gas flame. "Hot, hot," I said, just as one might do with a toddler.

One of his early creations was a chocolate concoction: One can of chocolate icing, a big bag of M & Ms and several Tootsie Rolls and Hershey Peanut Buttercups, all mixed together. Actually he couldn't eat it, because chocolate is a definite no-no for someone with a behavioral disorder; but I let him have a small amount as a treat. Most of his culinary creations were something for him to admire rather than to eat.

One of Corky's favorite dishes is macaroni and cheese with Brussels sprouts, which he can now make quite well. He also likes pork and beans, and fried chicken. I consider his chicken even better than KFC's. He learned recipes quickly; after making a dish once, all I had to do was set out the ingredients, and he proceeded like a grandmother who has spent her whole life in the kitchen.

He had learned to use salt sparingly, and I was thankful that his salt problem seemed to have resolved itself.

Our summer in the trailer was over all too quickly, and we had to return to Akron. But I felt Corky had taken giant steps in learning how to become self-sufficient.

His self-inflicted pain was still a problem. He cut his nails down to the quick and then put merthiolate on his fingertips. He slapped himself. He pulled on his lower lip, and tapped his forehead repeatedly. I massaged him and petted him when these actions continued. Then I began telling him, "Do it again. Slap yourself again." This was to him an unexpected reaction. Gradually he stopped hurting himself.

Corky knew by the time he entered his teens that he had a daddy somewhere in the city. "My daddy's name is Yummy," he would announce, to no one in particular, referring to John's nickname.

There was never any emotional connection between Corky and his dad. In fact, since the day I left John when Corky was a baby, the two had never laid eyes on each other. But a day came when I decided they should meet. I laid my plans carefully.

I knew that John's mother always had her entire family over to her house on Christmas. I primed Corky, then fifteen, that we were going to Grandma Florence's house and he would meet his daddy. I bought him an expensive suit for the occasion, and wrapped a bottle of Giorgio Cologne For Men that Corky was to present to John. When we arrived, I let Corky enter the house first while I lingered by the front door.

All heads swiveled as Corky marched up to his grandmother.

"It's Corky," she told the assembled guests. "Here's your daddy, Corky. Say hello to your daddy."

"Look, Yummy, here's your son," said another family member.

"Don't he look nice!"

"He looks just like you, Yummy."

The comments continued while Corky gravely approached his dad, extended his hand, which was solemnly shaken, and handed him the wrapped cologne. I watched John closely to gauge his reaction. His jaw dropped in shock. His eyes swept the room, hoping someone would come to his rescue. He knew he should say something, but he didn't know what. His eyes came to rest on me, still standing by the front door, and he finally mumbled, "You got that boy dressed real nice."

We stayed for only a short while. I tried to chitchat with several of the family, but I felt no closeness to any of them, with the exception of John's sister Beverly - the only one who had ever been kind to me.

I was satisfied, however. Corky had acquitted himself well. He never knew what that day meant to me. I wanted all of them to see that I was doing a good job raising my son, and that even with his handicap, he was capable of interacting with others to a limited extent, and had learned how to behave in public. I wanted to show them that I was holding my own, that I had done all this myself, with never a smidgen of support from any of their family or my own, either emotional or financial.

Corky's learning to become a gentleman was important for him as well as for me. To this end, I suggested he ask a young lady out for an evening. His first date was with a girl named Vanessa, who was fifteen, like Corky. She wore a black and white lacy dress for the big evening, and Corky looked very spiffy in white slacks and a silk shirt.

They went to the Brown Derby, a popular restaurant, for dinner, and then to an Eddie Murphy movie. I drove them, of course. Corky opened the car door for his date to get in, and seeing that her skirt was hanging outside the door frame, he carefully lifted it onto the seat.

That gesture really touched me; it showed how considerate Corky could be.

The two of them ordered their meal, and I slipped Corky a few bills to pay the check. Of course I had to finance his dates, but I let Corky deal with waitresses and cashiers so that he would gain experience in handling money. I gave them privacy while they ate so that they could talk without restraint. In the meantime I walked around the mall and window-shopped. I was really proud of how Corky conducted himself that evening.

Frank could also see that Corky was developing social skills and becoming more responsible.

"What do you think about getting a dog for Corky?" Frank asked me. "Do you think he can handle having a pet?"

"I think that would be wonderful. It would give him something he can talk to, without having to remember to look someone in the eye. And it will help him develop compassion for other living things."

Frank brought over a mixed-breed puppy that we named Brownie. He was golden-brown, part Labrador retriever, with floppy ears and a silky tail. The pup scampered over our living room carpet to where Corky was sitting, and licked his hand.

I explained to Corky that he would have to take Brownie outside every day, but since we had a fenced-in back yard, that didn't seem a problem. After three weeks, Corky was deeply attached to the dog. He wrestled with him, petted him, talked to him in a limited way, such as "Stop", "Eat, dog, eat!" or "oh-oh!" if the pup had an accident in the house. I was pleased that Corky took to the dog so readily.

In those days Corky's cousin Donald used to come over frequently. He was a year younger than Corky, and I encouraged his visits, hoping that Donald would prove to be a good playmate for Corky. But it seemed to me that Donald was always jealous of Corky, thinking he had more toys.

One day Corky and Donald were playing with Brownie in the back yard while I was at the store. For some unknown reason, Donald opened the gate, and Brownie shot out as though he had spied a rabbit. There was a screech of brakes, a thud, and then a red Taurus sped off.

When I came back from the store, a limp golden-brown shape lay at the curb. Brownie had been killed instantly.

"What happened?" I screamed.

"I didn't mean to let him out," Donald explained. "I opened the gate just a crack." He spoke without emotion, not the least bit remorseful.

"You killed Corky's dog!" I screamed at him. "You're never comin' over here again. Now go on home!"

I had been so happy that Corky had got attached to a living creature, and was finally capable of loving something. And now that something was taken away. How would Corky handle that?

I gathered the dog up in my arms and carried him to the back yard. I had Corky dig a hole to bury him in.

"Brownie is in dog heaven," I told Corky. He understood that Brownie wouldn't be there anymore to lick his hand, or greet him with a wagging tail like a metronome set on Presto.

We buried Brownie to the accompaniment of a sorrowful reading of the Twenty-third Psalm. We'd had him for just eight months.

For several days, Corky expressed the sadness he was feeling. "Poor Brownie, poor Brownie!" he kept repeating. Then the memory of Brownie faded from his consciousness.

Chapter 15

Long ago, I discovered that older white men often approach a black woman with the idea "I want to experience a little brown sugar before I die." Mostly they are just lonely and eager for some conversation and laughs. For the most part, my response has been, "I can't totally accommodate you, but we can be friends." So we talk, and I tell them about Corky, and upon leaving, they hand me a few bills, saying, "Here's a little something for you and Corky." I regard these men as gentle, kind-hearted, innocent types, not necessarily with lust in their hearts.

One of these men was a Mormon I called Farmer Fred. He was a jolly dumpling of a man, like a Santa Claus without the beard. He used to come and watch me dance at various nightclubs in Columbus, dressed in his customary bib overalls.

He lived on several thousand acres, where he raised beef cattle, chickens, soybeans, and corn, and made maple syrup to sell. He had a wife and several children, but I never met them. They would have frowned on his friendship with me. In addition, his Mormon religion disapproved of frequenting nightclubs. His wife, I'm sure, would have objected to the fifty dollar tips he surreptitiously slipped me.

Whenever he walked into the nightclub, the other performers alerted me: "Marty, here comes your Farmer Fred." After my act, I would go and sit at his table and order pizza.

"You look pretty tonight," he often said, as he gave me a hug. He would take my hand and stroke it gently, then discreetly slip a twenty or fifty dollar bill into it.

He was such a kind, generous person - I felt completely safe with him. In fact, I felt honored to be in his company.

"What's new on the farm?" I would ask him. I had always lived in a city, and had no idea how much back-breaking work farming involved.

"Well, the corn's comin' up, and one of the cows is about to have her calf." He loved farming, and he loved telling me what went on each season of the year. We sat there, munching pizza and sipping cokes, until closing time.

73

After about two years of these visits, I started inviting him to stay overnight at my Columbus apartment. I knew he was harmless, and nothing untoward would happen. One time I did ask him, "How can you stay away all night while your wife is at home?"

"My wife thinks I'm at a farmers' meeting," he responded with a sly smile.

Once, while his wife was away visiting relatives, he invited me and Corky to visit his farm. This gave Corky an opportunity to see cows close up. I took his hand and had him feel a warm, newly-laid egg. Farmer Fred let him feed the chickens, showing him how to throw the kernels into the pen. Corky laughed at the piglets jostling each other to nurse at their mother's teats, and at the huge pigs wallowing in the mud outside the barn. He threw a pebble at a cow to get its attention, but it ignored us and continued grazing.

Fred allowed us to ride his only horse, a reddish-brown mare. Both of us climbed onto her back, Corky in front of me, and the horse paced leisurely around the perimeter of the farm, skirting the wheat field where golden stalks bent in the breeze. Then the horse took us past the corn field, where we could see ripening ears on each tall green tasseled stalk. In the distance, one lone deer watched us cautiously, ready to bolt into the woods if our mount ventured into its safety zone. It was a wonderful day for me as well as for Corky.

In other ways, also, Farmer Fred was very kind to me. He brought hunks of cheese and cartons of eggs to my home. On these occasions I always cooked dinner for him. One year he mailed me a cake for my birthday. This pleasant platonic relationship continued for about five years.

A friendship of this sort is not unusual among African-American women. Ever since the early days of slavery in America, individual white men have done kind things for African-American women of their acquaintance, either secretly or openly. This goes on even today. The women have learned to be discreet about it, or they will be punished by their peers.

My friendship with Joe, the maintenance man, was not of that sort, however. He had an eighty-one-year-old mother in Columbus who lived in a large frame house filled with massive furniture and lots of German and Dutch antiques that had been in her family for generations. When she got sick, Joe asked me to help out at her house two days a week. Corky was in good hands with Frank, so I accepted Joe's offer.

Miss Violet was a small plump woman with white hair, twinkly blue eyes, and a small turned-up nose. I did her shopping, dusted and vacuumed, fixed her meals, and gave her baths. In fine weather I set her outside in the sun. She loved to tell me the history of each item in her home. At an earlier time in her life she had bought and sold antiques, but now the remainder of her artifacts were scattered throughout her house.

"This is from the early eighteen-hundreds," she told me, pointing to a small chest of drawers with brass drawer pulls. "This belonged to my grandma's grandpa." She handed me a pocket watch with gold filigree around the edges. "This is a Faberge bowl...This is a Bavaria plate. A dealer offered my fifty dollars for it, but I decided I didn't want to part with it. This bottle is a Lalique..."

In this way I learned a lot about antiques. I marveled that Miss Violet could remember the details about each piece. Mostly I was content to just look at them; I didn't want to risk dropping any.

After several months with Miss Violet, I had to cut back on my time in Columbus because a situation developed that required my presence in Akron. Whenever a friend or a neighbor was in trouble, I could not remain an idle onlooker, especially if there were children involved. I can't stand to see little kids suffer, so I jump in, take charge, and do whatever has to be done.

In some parts of town, the breakup of families, drug use, and violence had become as common as the robins hunting worms on every patch of grass. Individuals approached me to take advantage of my strength and my generosity. I was seen as a sturdy oak, a tower of tenacity, who can weather the fiercest storms. Those characteristics got me involved with Shirley's family, who lived across the street from me.

Shirley was hooked on drugs, and one day took off for Florida, leaving her three children with their stepfather, a loud, boisterous man, whose source of income was pimping. I became the contact person between the kids and their mother, the only link through whom they could communicate. Shirley sent me money every other month to use for the children's needs. Evidently she didn't trust the stepfather to refrain from squandering the money on himself. So I purchased food for the children, and clothing as the need arose, and paid the phone bills that rose into the stratosphere, due to Shirley's collect calls. My phone rang at unpredictable hours; I put the receiver down, ran across the street, told the kids, "Come, your mom wants to talk to you, get some clothes on" (if they were already in bed.) I hustled them over to my house and let them talk, each of the three in turn. It made them happy to talk to their mother, who otherwise remained unreachable; that was important to me. I hugged the children and gave them words of encouragement: "You mom will be coming back soon", though I had no inkling when that might happen.

The months stretched into years. Six years passed before Shirley saw fit to come back.

I tried my best to save Shirley's children, but there is only so much one individual can do for a dysfunctional family. Shirley, the children's stepfather, and the oldest child all ended up in prison.

Chapter 16

Frank was used to dealing with Corky for extended periods while I was away in Columbus. However, one time it was not dancing engagements or Miss Violet that kept me away. It was my generosity and implicit trust in people that got me into a heap of trouble.

One of my dancing acquaintances in Columbus was Cindy, a tall white girl, the same size as me, who wore her thick blonde hair in an Afro. I knew she was going with a black guy, who got her into some sort of trouble, for which she was sent to jail. I think her boyfriend had kicked her out of his apartment by that time.

The day of her release from prison, she came to my apartment.

"Marty, I just got out of jail, and I need a bath real bad. Can I use your place to clean up?"

Of course I let her in, ran a bath for her, gave her bubble bath and shampoo, and left her alone to soak. Then I gave her brand new panties, a slip, one of my dresses, a pair of my shoes, and a little purse into which I tucked a five-dollar bill.

"You need a good meal," I told her. "I'll fix you a dinner. Do you want to do your nails? And here, put a dab of this on." I handed her my Mary Kay nail polish and my bottle of Chanel 22. Then I went into the kitchen and put a steak on the grill for her.

She looked ready for an evening on the town when she sat down to eat.

"I really appreciate all this, Marty," she said between mouthfuls.

She had barely started on the steak when the phone rang. It was Joe.

"Can you come over to my mother's? She fell and can't get up, and I need some help."

"All right. I'll be there right away."

I explained to Cindy that I had to leave, but would be back in about a half-hour.

I was thankful that Miss Violet didn't seem to have any broken bones. Apparently she'd had a dizzy spell and passed out. Luckily she didn't hit her head on any furniture. Joe and I raised her and got her seated on the couch. She assured us she was all right again. Joe

77

said he would stay with her for a while, but told me I didn't have to, so I hurried back to my apartment.

Upon my return, I saw the empty plate on the kitchen counter, but no sign of Cindy. Alarm bells went off in my head. I ran to the bedroom, where I suddenly remembered I had cash stashed away in my jewelry box. I flipped the lid open. My eyes took in the sparkling earrings, the silver and turquoise rings, the beads and necklaces. But no cash. Gone - all $480! So that was the way she repaid my kindness!

I stewed over my loss for two days. On the third day, I happened to spy Cindy in the supermarket. She was with her black boyfriend, with whom she'd evidently made up. I followed them discreetly, wondering what I should do. What audacity, I thought, to do her shopping so close to the scene of her crime! To add to my disgust and anger, I saw they had packages of shrimp and lobster in their basket.

The boyfriend turned into the Heat and Eat aisle, while Cindy entered the Household Products aisle. In the middle of that aisle I went into action. I "did a kangaroo" on her - jumped her with fists flying and feet kicking. She fell against a display rack, sending boxes of detergent tumbling all around us.

"Help, Michael, help me!" she called.

"How can you steal from the hand that feeds you, you dirty bitch?" I screamed.

Michael came running and tried to separate us. I kept hammering at her face, while I yelled at him, "She's feedin' you with MY money!" I stopped beating her up when I saw blood dripping from her face.

By this time the manager had called the police, who responded quickly. Two policemen subdued me and led me out to the paddy wagon. We drove to the police station, where I was booked for assault.

I decided to cooperate with the police from here on. I knew everyone in the justice system would see the incident as a racial thing - a black girl and a white girl fighting over a black man.

I was put into a holding cell, and three days later I bailed myself out. I had already called a lawyer I knew, who frequented the nightclub where I danced. He was an older, heavy-set man with a small neat beard and dark-framed glasses on a round face.

During my appointment at his office, I told him my story, and added, "I'm not just a dancer, I'm more than that. Here are some of my credentials." I showed him my newspaper write-up from Las Vegas and some of my song lyrics.

On my day in court, Cindy showed up sporting a black eye that contrasted with her pale complexion, and a neck collar; it seemed I had broken her collar bone. Her boyfriend arrived somewhat later, eliciting an adoring "Oh, Michael, you came!" from her.

Oh hell, I thought, that blows my case out of the water. Now for sure they'll regard this as a simple case of jealousy.

Cindy testified against me, telling the jury how I had, with no provocation, attacked her in the store. Upon cross-examination, she admitted stealing my money.

Then my lawyer presented his argument.

"She's not a violent person," he told the court. "Sing, Marty!"

So I gave my best rendition of "Who Can I Turn To" to a hushed courtroom. Everyone listened respectfully until I finished the entire song.

I had three charges against me: assault, destruction of property, and resisting arrest. The last two were dismissed, but I couldn't get out of the assault charge. In the end I was sentenced to twenty days in the women's workhouse, reduced to seventeen because I had already been held three days.

Psychologically, being sent to jail gave me a horrible feeling. I was not a criminal; why should I be locked up alongside women who were child abusers, con artists, embezzlers, or worse? I don't belong here, I kept thinking. What if word gets out to the various nightclubs, and they all blackball me? However, I was determined to make the best of it. The only person in Akron that knew the truth was Corky's Aunt Beverly. I called and asked her to look after Corky while I was away. Frank and my own family never knew. Frank was used to my being in Columbus anyway, so I made up a story to explain why I couldn't come back to Akron for the next three weeks. I called Corky every two or three days to let him know I was thinking of him.

Of course I also had to tell my boss at the nightclub, who was very understanding. He agreed to hold my place open until I returned. And I had to tell Miss Violet that I couldn't come to her house for the next three weeks.

The Women's Workhouse was a one-floor building, like a dormitory or an army barracks, with a pervasive smell of bleach. It held 25 or 30 women. Each of us had one of the double-bunk beds, and each had a housekeeping job to do. Mine was cleaning the bathroom.

I had taken my notebook that goes practically everywhere with me, in which I write song lyrics as ideas come to me. Upon arrival at the workhouse, they took the notebook and my pencil away.

"You can't do that," I protested. "What do you think I'm going to do with the pencil - stab somebody?" My equipment was returned to me grudgingly. While the other women visited among one another and did their chores, I sat on my bed and wrote songs. Once or twice I sat outside in the sunshine when we were allowed outdoors.

I discovered the bathroom had excellent acoustics, especially when the showers were running. Between the steam and the tile walls echoing my voice, my songs sounded great, and so I did my cleaning chores while singing my heart out.

In the evenings, I serenaded the other women arrayed on their bunk beds with spirituals and such numbers as Summertime, Moon River, and I Could Have Danced All Night.

That escapade cost me close to $1500 - a $500 fine and $500 court costs, in addition to what I lost to Cindy.

I know I overreacted. I could have taken Cindy to Small Claims Court to recover my loss. I told myself I have to stop being too good to people. It's my nature to be generous - I'm a giving and sharing kind of person. I believe that what you give, you get back three times over. This time it didn't work out that way. I needed to be more selective, and observe limitations in what and to whom I give. It was a lesson that has stayed with me.

Several weeks after my jail term, Miss Violet became bedridden. I now had to carry her, or push her in a wheelchair. She became subdued, and some of the sparkle left her blue eyes. I took to playing tapes of Indian music to make a relaxing atmosphere for her.

I knew she had grandchildren somewhere, but in all the time I cared for her, I never laid eyes on them. As far as I knew, she never received a card or letter or phone call from any of them either.

Her diabetes got worse, and the doctors decided her leg needed amputation. Unfortunately, she passed away peacefully in the hospital.

It fell to me to make funeral arrangements, with input from her son Joe. I ordered lavender roses, that being her favorite color. And I asked Dwaine, an old friend in Akron, to come to Columbus to help me.

I had first met Dwaine many years before, at one of my day jobs. He worked hard as a chef, waiter, and bartender, and I always felt he should have a restaurant of his own. I was drawn to him because of his kindness, intelligence, and balanced personality. He encouraged me in my singing and dancing, and became one of my chief boosters. Whenever one of my songs was played on any of the northern Ohio college radio stations, Dwaine was the first to call in and ask "Please play that Marty Diamond song again." Our relationship remained platonic. I saw him go through several relationships with other women, and I gave him advice when he asked for it. He was popular with women, perhaps too much so, and I think he was afraid to commit to any one woman. I knew that if I was ever in a jam, Dwaine would come to my rescue. Frank, I knew, would be unable to come to Columbus. His machine shop needed him, and Corky needed him, and I certainly did not want Corky in Columbus at this time, even if Frank felt that he could get away.

So Dwaine accompanied me to the funeral. The day was cool and foggy; dampness clung to our faces and clothes. The casket was being lowered into the ground, and the minister was intoning the final benediction, when a dilapidated van pulled into the cemetery and about fifteen people spilled out, like numerous circus clowns popping out of a tiny car. Under different circumstances, I would have laughed.

Eyeing them, Dwaine murmured in my ear, "Oh, my God, them hillbillies gonna shoot you in the back 'cause they think you gon' take their grandma's house."

I tensed in alarm. The men all looked like biker types - ponytails and heavy beards, jeans and leather jackets over T-shirts. The women likewise wore jeans and T-shirts, or denim skirts. Their looks and demeanor made me certain they had a gun in their van. One of the women, young and highly pregnant, detached herself and ran towards me. Without a word, she fell on me in an embrace. At that moment the sun popped out from behind a veil of clouds, like a signal of approval from above. She clung to me for several minutes, and the idea darted through my mind that maybe she was protecting me from any mischief planned by the men.

"You should have come to see your grandma before she died," I said gently.

Guilt, remorse, and sorrow brought on a cascade of tears that spilled down my shoulder.

"It's all right," I said. "Go ahead and cry. You'll feel better." I patted her on the back. Her tears gradually subsided.

"Thank you for all you done for grandma," she finally said, lifting her head to look at my face. I smiled at her. "Your grandma was a great lady, a tough lady."

The rest of the clan, believing this woman to be their spokesperson, never said a word to me.

Chapter 17

I was getting fewer dancing engagement; younger dancers were pushing older ones like me out of jobs. Each time I was onstage, waves of happiness surged over me, especially now, knowing these occasions came less often. Dancing gave me dignity, it gave a purpose to my life - other than raising my son, of course. The spotlight was always hot and blinding in my eyes as I moved to the music, slow and seductive at first, then gradually quickening to a steady beat. I imagined the upturned faces and staring eyes beyond the footlights. The last time this occurred was at a stag party in 1991, though I didn't know it would be my farewell performance. I was then forty-four years old, but the years had been kind to me. It was gratifying that I could still entrance an audience. I heard one man announce to his buddies, "She can have my wallet, my driver's license, my car keys, any time!" For a brief moment I was again the center of the universe. Then it was over and darkness enveloped me. Usually, soon after my exit, darkness wrapped itself around my heart also, as all the problems at home broke into my consciousness. Why did my life have to be so difficult? Did other people have problems too, that at times seemed to overwhelm them? Now and then the sturdy oak that I appeared to be to others came close to cracking.

Fewer dance gigs gave me more time with Corky, supervising his daily activities. To get Corky to do what I wanted, whether it was chores around the house or good behavior on the outside, I used potato chips or bits of fruit, and later, money as incentives. Then, in his late teens, I phased out money and substituted hugs and kisses, because I wanted him to feel self-satisfied and proud of doing something well, without thought of compensation.

One day I ladled out peas, potatoes, and his favorite fried chicken pieces onto his plate. He took the salt shaker and began shaking it vigorously until a thick layer of salt covered each course.

"That's too much salt, Corky," I said. "You know that's not good for you."

He looked at me, then turned his attention back to his plate and shook more salt onto it.

"Corky, that's too much salt!" My voice rose to a scream. "You can't eat that!"

He rose from his chair, his face contorted like a Nerf ball squished out of shape, and took a step towards me. He was a full-grown adult now, weighing close to two hundred pounds.

"You want to hit me, don't you," I burst out. It was more of a statement than a question.

"Yeah!"

"Well, go ahead. Hit me!"

His fist shot out and caught me under the chin. I crumpled to the floor as all the lights went out in my head.

About fifteen minutes later I came to. Corky was sitting at the table, looking scared, his food untouched.

I went to the phone and called the police. When an officer arrived, I met him at the door.

"My son just hit me and knocked me out. I want you to handcuff him, take him into your cruiser, and drive around with him for about ten minutes. Then you can bring him home."

The policeman did as I asked. Upon returning, he walked Corky to the front door and said, "Now don't you ever hit your mom again!" He shook Corky's hand and left.

A much chastened Corky said, "Mommy, let's kiss and make up." I knew he felt really bad about the incident. But I think I handled it the right way.

Corky still had a few things to learn about handling money. For his eighteenth birthday, he received seven or eight dollars. With the bills pinned to his shirt, he set off for the supermarket to spend his gift money. But in the parking lot, a man approached him, ripped the bills away, and ran. Corky returned home, visibly upset; his facial expression changed from dejected to angry. Without any prompting on my part, he called the police and told them calmly what happened. Of course there was no way to recover the money.

"That's life," I told him. "It's all part of life. People will take your money if they get a chance. Next time, keep your money in your pocket."

It was a good lesson for him, probably worth the seven or eight dollars that he lost.

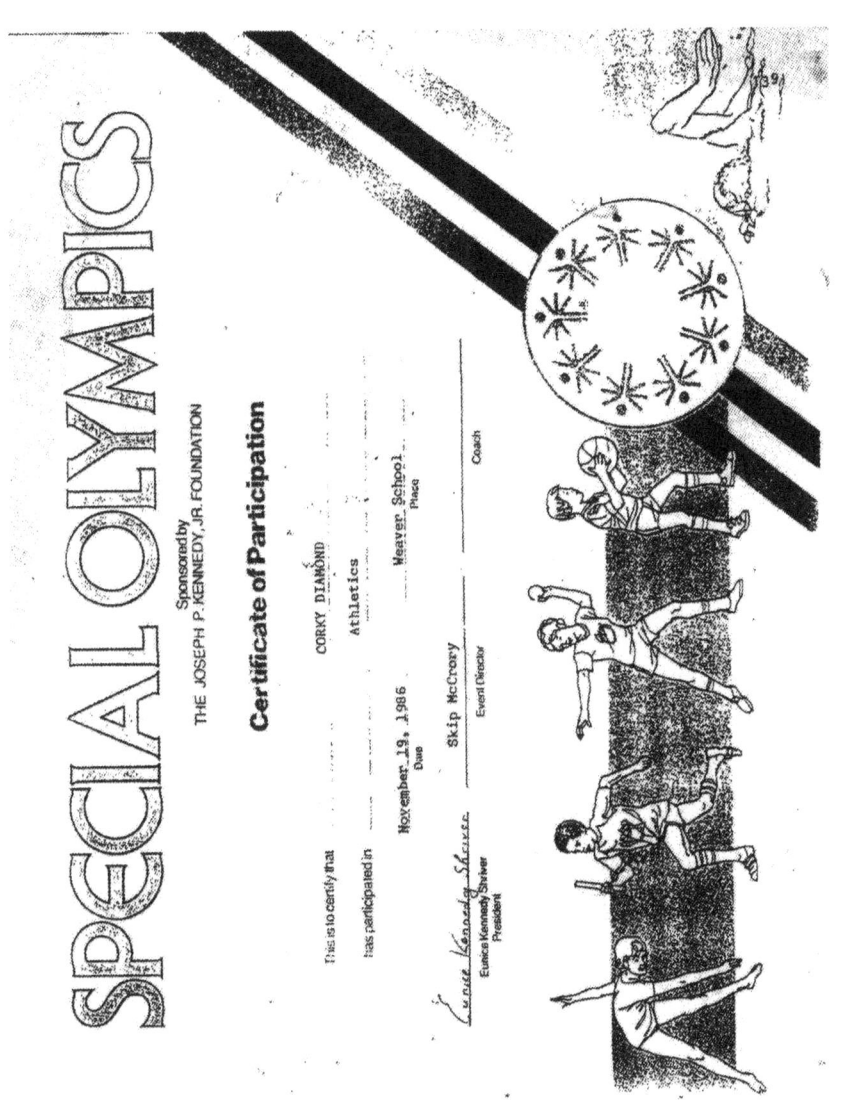

Skill-Courage-Sharing-Joy

CORKY DIAMOND

is a Special Olympian who has participated in the

WEAVER SCHOOL/HIGH SCHOOL - SW

Special Olympics Program

Eunice Kennedy Shriver
EUNICE KENNEDY SHRIVER
Chairman of the Board
Special Olympics, Inc.

R. SARGENT SHRIVER
President
Special Olympics, Inc.

November 16, 1988
Date

Understanding numbers, and addition and subtraction were skills Corky gained mostly from TV programs. Our TV was on for much of the day, whenever Corky was home. He liked The Price Is Right, Wheel of Fortune, and Jeopardy, not because of any intellectual challenge, but because of the numbers on the screen: $200, $400, $1000, $2000, etc. He had learned simple arithmetic at Weaver School, but the main things Weaver taught Corky were sociability, writing, and swimming. His class did some form of physical exercise each day. By the time he reached his teens, he was well-coordinated. He especially loved the trampoline, and got very good at doing seat drops and knee drops. Team games didn't interest him much; he preferred solitary activities, like roller skating, running and jumping, shot put, downhill skiing, and bicycling on a stationary bike.

At fourteen, the school taught him simple office procedures, like filing and working the copy machine. From then on, he helped out in the school office. I begged the school to give him academic courses. "Please put him on a computer, let him learn to work a computer," I asked repeatedly. They never did.

I always felt the school gave white students more help and assistance. Perhaps they believed there was more potential there.

Corky's teachers and coaches expected a lot from him, because he was a big boy, always tall for his age. He couldn't always perform up to their expectations, and this led to frustration. Even now he hates to make a mistake at anything.

I had taken Corky to swimming pools from an early age, and he had developed a paddling stroke with a technique all his own. As he entered his teens, the swimming teacher at Weaver began working with Corky to perfect his strokes. Corky liked swim class; it brought a happy smile to his face, and he exchanged comments with the other children in a cheerful, high-pitched voice.

In time he got to be a good enough swimmer to represent Weaver at many swim meets. Usually he brought home at least one trophy or medal from these meets. The swim competition did wonders in boosting his self-confidence. But if he didn't win, he was not particularly concerned.

I have mixed feelings about Weaver School. Although the staff did a lot for Corky, I feel they could have done more. On a more personal level, the school cost me $1500 indirectly.

Corky had a beautiful leather jacket that cost $300. One day at school he found it all cut up; someone had taken a knife blade or scissors and slashed it in numerous places. I marched into the principal's office with the ruined jacket and demanded to have the culprit found, and to be reimbursed. Some half-hearted attempts were made, but the perpetrator was never found. The jacket hung in the principal's office for months and was finally removed and, I presume, discarded.

The Special Olympics of 1990-91 also cost me a bundle. Corky was in Columbus, competing in swimming events. All the Weaver students were staying at a dorm on the Ohio State campus. It was a stormy day; the rain came down as though God had planned to hit the earth with another deluge.

Disregarding the weather, I decided to drive down to Columbus. I wanted to give Corky some spending money and his favorite baseball cap. I also wanted to pat him on the back and give him words of encouragement.

I was stopped at the entrance to the dorm.

"No, you can't see him," I was told. "You'll have to leave."

I persisted. The staff people were adamant. I got hysterical. Finally, seeing that I was getting nowhere, I left. It was late, and I needed to either head home, or find a place to spend the night. I got into my car and floored the accelerator.

I never saw the truck coming at me. There was a screech of metal scraping metal, then an ominous silence. The truck driver and I got out to survey the damage. Each vehicle looked like a survivor of a demolition derby. Luckily neither of us was injured.

Too upset to go farther, I decided to sleep in my car. Next morning I awoke to find several young white faces peering curiously at my supine form. I shooed them away and gunned the motor to get me home. It was fortunate that my car was in drivable condition.

Of course the referee in traffic court found me negligent and ordered me to pay for the damage to the truck. Together with my own car repair, the cost came to $1200. I still hold Weaver School responsible for the accident.

Whenever Corky was out alone, we had to rely on his guardian angel to watch over him. However, when he and I went somewhere together, I could protect him. I was as fierce and unrestrained about this as a mother bear protecting her cubs. Usually it was smart-alecky kids that tried to torment him.

We were at a roller rink one day; Corky skated happily while I watched from the sidelines, when one young man decided he was going to do something to gain attention and possibly admiration from his buddies: He tripped Corky as he was skating, and Corky toppled like a felled oak tree. He picked himself up, unhurt and unaware of what had caused him to fall, and continued skating merrily. But I was sizzling inside.

For three hours, until closing time, I kept my fury bottled up. Then, before leaving, I approached the young punk.

"I'm Corky's mom. I saw you trip Corky. If you ever, ever do it again, I'll cut your dick off!"

The fellow looked at me in amazement. Possibly no one had ever stood up to him before. He managed a mumbled, "I'm sorry, I won't do it again," and hurried off to join his buddies.

Then something happened that was to keep Corky from ever skating again.

It was a May afternoon when my phone rang. I was home alone, Corky having walked to the barbershop.

"You'd better come to the barbershop right away," said a voice. "Corky was hit by a car at the corner."

Hit by a car! The words reverberated in my head. I slammed down the phone and ran for my car keys. My tires squealed as I backed out of the driveway and onto the street. What's happened to my punkin, I wondered. As panic rose in me, an unrelenting pounding mounted in my chest. Hadn't I taught him ever so carefully to look both ways before crossing a street, to watch the traffic lights, to gauge whether he had enough time to cross before a light changed?

I figured it was bound to happen sooner or later. All I could do was hope for the best, and pray that he wasn't hurt too badly.

I saw him sitting at the curb as I approached. He was holding his leg at an odd angle. Thank God, I thought, he's conscious; maybe it's just a broken leg.

The ambulance was already there, and Corky calmly gave the paramedics his name. The police were there too, and an officer was talking to the young man whose gray Honda had hit Corky while making a right turn.

I screamed at him, "How could you have done that? How could you have hurt my son like that?"

The policeman determined that the driver was not at fault, and let him go. It turned out he had no insurance, anyway.

Corky's leg was pretty badly mangled. I watched the paramedics lift him carefully onto a gurney and slide it into their vehicle.

"I'm comin' with you," I announced. "You're not leavin' me here. I'm his mother. Let me get in the back with him."

"No, not in the back. If you want to come along, sit up front by the driver."

I guess they didn't trust what I might do, as hysterical as I was.

I waited with rising apprehension at the hospital emergency room. Finally someone came and said, "It looks like his leg is broken in two places. The surgeon is going to set it and we'll keep him here for several days."

Corky stayed in the hospital ten days, and I never left his bedside except to grab a bite to eat. The nurses let me sleep on the armchair in his room. All that constant sitting made my feet swell up like two cantaloupes. Corky's father showed up one day to pay a quick nonchalant visit at his bedside. Word must have gotten to him, and he thought it was something he was supposed to do, just for the sake of appearances.

I massaged Corky's back and his good leg, and I did a lot of praying. Once an intern came in and said he needed to insert a catheter in Corky. I shrieked at him, "What do you want to do that for? Ain't no way you're gonna mess with his thingy-dingy! Leave it alone!"

I figured Corky had gone through enough pain and discomfort already, without having to undergo catheterization. Besides, he had voided just a short time before.

The doctor retreated, somewhat taken aback. Probably no one had ever talked to him like that. Most people think doctors are the closest thing to God; but I had my own opinion of what they should and should not do to my son.

Corky came home with a steel pin in his leg. I'm sure he was more careful in crossing streets after that. Sometimes I ask him when he's ready to leave the house, "Are you gonna get hit by a car?"

"Oh, no, no!"

Certainly it was an experience he doesn't want to repeat, although I must say he handled it much better than I did.

A different kind of protection was something I needed to teach Corky. He already knew and accepted the anatomical differences between men and women, and he knew that Mommy wears different kinds of underwear than he does. A few years previously I had asked him, "Did anyone ever touch you down there when you were a little boy?"

"No. Anyone ever touch you when you were a little girl?"

His echoing statements could get on my nerves at times. But I got the message across that there are appropriate and inappropriate ways of touching another person. Years later, he told me there had been one homosexual advance, but, as he put it, "I made him stop!"

Now, at age twenty or twenty-one, I decided Corky needed further sex education. He might some day find himself in a situation where a woman would take advantage of his innocence, and I wanted him to be prepared for such an eventuality.

I purchased a cucumber and some condoms.

"This is what you do if you ever make love to a woman," I said as I rolled the condom over the cucumber. I had him practice doing it, while explaining that, when the time came, he was to use the condom on himself, NOT on a cucumber. As far as I know, he has never had to put that lesson into practice.

True to my belief that Corky was about ten years behind in certain aspects of his development, puberty was completed at age twenty-three. His voice had deepened about three years before.

"Big one, Momma," he would say in the mornings, showing me the erection he woke up with. I told him he might stroke it in the bathroom until the 'big one' went away, "but if you do that every day," I warned, "it will fall off."

Corky was now fairly self-sufficient. He could cook, clean, and shop. If necessary, he could get along for several days without me or Frank.

Chapter 18

A good portion of my money always went for Corky's care. But occasionally I indulged myself and spent a bundle on something of no practical use, simply because I wanted to.

I had entered my song "Love" in a national contest for songwriters, and I was thrilled when it won a ninth place in the contemporary jazz category, out of thousands of entries. I also had a new man in my life. Ronald was an electrical engineer who was taking additional courses at night. That indication of ambition, together with his handsome features, attracted me. After several dates, I knew I was in love - again. He had another girlfriend somewhere, but I didn't care. I wanted to celebrate my love for him, to make our relationship memorable, and so I asked him to be in a video with me, using my prize-winning song as the sound track.

I knew just the setting I wanted - the gray stone building in Alliance known as the Morgan Castle. The Morgans were probably the leading industrial family of Alliance, having founded the Morgan Engineering Company, makers of hydraulic machines, traveling cranes, and other heavy machinery, and after that, Solid Steel Company, the forerunner of American Steel Foundries. The castle is set on lovely park-like grounds. It is now owned by the school administration, which uses it for offices.

I hired a commercial crew for my video. Three camera men and I drove down together, along with props I wanted to use - a small table, an enormous roasted turkey, and a lemon-yellow bicycle built for two. I wore a long white Victorian-style dress with a heart-shaped neckline.

As I waited for Ronald at the castle grounds, I remembered the Alliance of my childhood - a railroad town with machine shops, steel mills, and brick factories. I used to explore the town instead of going straight home when school let out. I especially liked hobnobbing with the hoboes that hung around the railroad tracks. One of them used to play mournful tunes on his harmonica, and the haunting sound stirred something deep inside me. Those tunes seemed to express all the misery in the world. Yet on the surface, the hoboes seemed happy, always ready to joke about their situation. I enjoyed being in their midst, ever eager to gather up sticks at the edge of the woods to feed the fire that heated their cans of beans, as my price of admission into their company. I wondered now if there were still hoboes over at the tracks.

I was afraid Ronald would get cold feet and not show up; I knew he wasn't crazy-in-love with me. Then what would I tell the camera crew, whom I had already paid an advance sum? When his brown Ford turned into the long curved driveway, it was as though the sun had come out and smiled upon me.

We set up our props, and the camera started rolling. It followed Ronald and me pedaling around the pastoral castle grounds, it focused on the ducks dabbling in the pond, it panned around the castle itself. I had Ronald kiss me for the camera, then he pulled my sleeve down a little and kissed me on my exposed shoulder. While the camera was focused on me, I lip-synched the song. I even commandeered an older couple who happened to be strolling around the grounds to be supporting actors in my production.

Back in Akron, at the video crew's studio, I helped them edit the footage. I ended up with a lovely video lasting three minutes and forty seconds to remember that August day when I was in love with Ronald. I never showed it to anyone, or sent it anywhere; it was for my eyes alone.

As I expected, the relationship with Ronald didn't last, but it was among the best I've had. I made myself get on with my life without him.

In 1990, I felt the time had come to make another attempt to bring my songs to the attention of people in the business. In October of that year, I decided to attend the disk jockeys' convention in Atlanta.

I had fifty demo tapes of my songs made up that I planned to hand out there. There was only one problem: I was short of money. But that did not deter me.

I had the cab driver in Atlanta let me off at the Marriott Hotel. Instead of walking in the front, I ambled around to the back door, where I found a security guard.

I put on a panicky tone of voice. "I've got a lot of luggage," I told the security guard. "I've been waiting for some guys to come down and help me with my bags. Will you watch my demo tapes while I go in and get the keys?" I handed him my silver hat box containing the

demo tapes. He let me in, and I took the elevator to the eighth floor. Waiters were setting up for a party in one large suite. I latched onto one big handsome black guy.

"Yo, bro man," I said to him. "I've snuck in here. I've got a security man holding my luggage downstairs. If you help me with my luggage, I can make it the rest of the way."

"Good for you, baby," he said. "You got this far. I'll help you."

He and I went downstairs, to the back door. I hugged the security guard and thanked him for watching my bags. The waiter escorted me back to the eighth floor, where he continued with his set-ups. I hid my two bags behind a couch.

"Fine as you is, you're not gonna have no problem," he assured me. "But I gotta go now."

I sat down, then found a ladies' room to freshen up in, and returned to watch as the crowd began to drift in. This was one of many parties going on, I found out. I stayed in my corner, keeping an eye on my luggage, but meeting people who happened to wander by. With each one, I asked myself, is this the one who might help me from here on?

I spied a DJ from Virginia and engaged him in conversation. I found him pleasant, and he was small enough that I could fight him off, should that become necessary.

"I need a place to keep my luggage and to sleep tonight," I told him. "Could I share your room?"

He agreed readily. "Will you take me up now and give me a key?" I continued.

So he took me and my bags to his room on the eleventh floor, and gave me his key, saying, "I can get another key from the desk."

It was now 9:30 p.m. I had arrived at the airport at 7 p.m., and already I was situated for the night. I returned to the party and began handing out my tapes, each of which contained three of my songs.

I acted like I belonged there, and before long, I felt I really did fit right in. The DJs came from all over the world; their name tags proclaimed London, Paris, Vienna, and other far-away places as their homes. I concentrated on the European DJs.

Other people at the party gave out tapes also. Some even gave tapes to me, assuming I was an artist.

I got back to the hotel room before my new-found friend. While waiting, I turned his bed down for him, as a signal that I had no intention of sleeping with him. I lit a bayberry candle, one of several I carried with me, and left one of my tapes on his pillow. Then I climbed under the covers of the other bed.

He returned to the room a little later. We talked for a while about the music business. He told me some DJs still accept money under the table to play certain songs, but he never engaged in that practice.

"For new artists, the college stations are the best way to get known," he advised me. "They play soft jazz and soft rock. You should get your songs out to them."

I could tell he was exhausted, so I turned to the wall to let him retire in privacy.

"Well, see you at breakfast in the morning," he said, and turned out the light.

I already knew what he told me about college radio stations. I succeeded in getting airplay at Kent State University, Mount Union College, and Bowling Green University.

After meeting DJs at their convention, I received postcards from Paris and Australia and three American towns saying the DJs there had played my tapes. It was gratifying to know that listeners in those far-away places had heard and enjoyed my songs.

Having indulged my desire to become known as a singer and songwriter, I was ready to engage in new activities, some of which brought me satisfaction, while others were to bring me only headaches.

Chapter 19

I have always liked old things: old houses, old-fashioned household skills like making jelly or candles or soap, old-fashioned clothing, old folks in their seventies and eighties, and mementos of bygone days.

Aunt Sarah, who taught me so many skills in my teens, molded my perspective and imprinted on me a love of anything old. I ended up being a bundle of paradoxes. On the one hand, I broke ground for African-Americans, being the first black dancer in Alliance and at Tall Paul's in Akron and the Astor Theater. On the other hand, I was attracted to the Victorian African-American look: high-necked cotton dresses and high-button shoes, and in addition, memorabilia of the black experience in America.

To indulge my passion for old things, I started gathering things that people put at the curb for trash collection - broken chairs, end tables, shelf units that could be painted or refinished, wicker furniture that needed repair. I loved bringing out the beauty of old wood - the uneven rings and concentric lines of the tree's growth pattern and the rich umber, sepia, or chestnut colors.

In refinishing or reconditioning furniture, I got help from a new man who had entered my life. I had met Sammy on a sultry August afternoon when I went to visit a girl friend and someone introduced us. He took my hand in a very gentle way, and our eyes met and held fast. The other people drifted away. Sammy and I wandered over to a nearby park, sat on the swings, and talked for the next three hours. This is the way it should be, I thought: a beautiful setting and someone I can open up my heart to.

The moon had climbed high into the dusky sky when we ambled slowly, as in a dream, back up the street. We parted, and I slowly floated down to earth again. My feet felt they had wings as I hurried home. Then, with a jolt, the thought hit me: Oh-oh, I'm doing it to Frank again. How would he react?

Of course he demanded to know where I had been. "Don't you remember, you were supposed to go out with me and Corky this evening?"

Usually even-tempered, he scowled and his voice rose in pitch like the siren of an approaching ambulance as he fussed at me. I really couldn't blame him, but on the other hand, I felt I was entitled to get together with friends occasionally, and possibly acquire a new black boyfriend. The only explanation I gave Frank was that I was having such a good time with my girl friends that I hated to leave, and the evening just slipped away.

Sammy started calling me, and we would meet at the park or the mall. He always made me laugh with funny stories and one-liners, and I would return home in a light-hearted mood, ready to talk to Corky about his activities of the day.

Whenever weather permitted, I put my reconditioned items in the driveway or the front yard, and a big sign near the curb saying YARD SALE. Using my knowledge of antiques that I had gained from Miss Violet, I recognized some of the items I salvaged from roadside trash as genuine antiques. I took these to dealers to get an idea what I should charge for them. I began studying books on antiques from the library, especially those dealing with black history, so that I could recognize items of value - anything considered a collector's item. I found out there is a market among African-Americans for containers or advertising posters with black faces on them, black dolls, etc., anything documenting black history.

Sammy saw me in my yard one afternoon stripping furniture. He took the brush out of my hand and finished the job. Then he repaired an end table with a broken leg. He seemed to know what he was doing, and he could work faster than I could. A rocking chair that he refinished for me sold for $100 at one of my yard sales. I was impressed with what Sammy could do.

I had a kidney-shaped table with a matching bench that I had rescued from its intended destination - the city's landfill. Sammy found some upholstery material, sat down at my sewing machine, and made covers for the two pieces. Then he sewed a pair of ruffled curtains and covered a wastebasket with the same material. That really blew my mind. How many men could undertake such projects and do a creditable job? As an encore, Sammy rewired a table lamp for me.

One afternoon Sammy and his brother Mark helped me put up lattice-work around my back patio. Sammy had brought his jigsaw over to cut two-by-fours. Corky watched us; we gave him a hammer, a piece of scrap wood, and some nails to let him think he was helping us. He banged away at the nails earnestly, his face a study in concentration.

Suddenly, while I was working, a lightning bolt of pain snaked through me.

"Help! I've cut my damn thumb off!"

My right thumb had got in the way of the blade, and the last joint was now hanging on by a thin sliver of skin. To stop the flow of blood, I grabbed it with my left hand and held it tightly in place.

"What the hell you doin'?" Sammy asked. "You always tryin' to do somethin' you ain't got no business doin'! You wanna go to the hospital?"

"Hell no, I can't afford no hospital."

I had emergency medical equipment in a metal box in Corky's room, which I had assembled while Corky was in the hospital waiting for his leg to mend. It was more than a first aid kit - more like a paramedic kit. I had Sammy bring that box to the kitchen table.

"Mark, get a bowlful of ice cubes ready. Corky, go get the bottles of peroxide and witch hazel and alcohol. Sammy, go look in the bathroom cabinet and bring me the Motrin."

I had Motrin pills left over from when I'd had a toothache. Two pills of 800 mg each should be enough for the present purpose, I decided.

"Corky, get me a glass of hot water and help me take two Motrins." After I had downed the pills, I had Corky pour peroxide, witch hazel, and alcohol onto the ice cubes. He must have used up half a bottle of each.

By this time, seven or eight minutes had passed since my accident. My thumb was now numb from being squeezed. When I felt myself getting drowsy from the Motrins, I dunked my thumb into the ice, moaning and whimpering as the pain returned. I held my thumb there until it turned white, then patted it gently with a clean towel dipped in hot water. Then I painted the edges of my wound with Betadine, iodine, and merthiolate, letting each one dry in turn. From my medical kit I took butterfly stitches, which are like tiny clamps, and placed twenty of those all around my thumb to hold it in place. Wrapping gauze around my thumb completed my operation.

Throughout all this, Corky watched and repeated, "Momma hurt her thumb, Momma hurt her thumb!" Was he overcome with feelings of sympathy? I wanted to believe that. It would mean that he had learned to empathize with others, to show compassion - in other words, that he was at last fully human.

My thumb healed in due time with only tiny scars that were almost invisible. In retrospect, I was surprised that I had remained so calm and level-headed. I guess I get hysterical only where Corky is concerned. I told Corky over and over, "You were such a great help to me when I hurt myself. I couldn't have done what I did without you! You're my hero!" I gave him a hug every time. I was immensely thankful that he was able to follow my commands, and do it quickly. Of course he always knew where everything was kept in my household. I never had to worry about misplacing anything. All I had to do was ask Corky, "Where is the Windex? Where is the box of envelopes?" and he'd tell me. If we ran out of something, he told me, or went out and purchased it himself. "Goin' to the store. Need laundry soap." He always had his own money, but I reimbursed him for what he spent for the household.

I made light of my thumb injury to Frank, telling him I had cut myself in the kitchen. If he knew the truth, he would have blamed Sammy for letting me handle the jigsaw, and I didn't want to cause trouble between the two. The friendship of each one meant a lot to me.

In the spring, Sammy planted a garden for me: tomatoes, beans, and cucumbers in the back, and petunias, marigolds, and primrose in the front. He continued helping me refinish furniture for my yard sales.

Customers and people that stopped only to browse at my sales told me, "You should have an antique store for all these lovely things."

When my house and garage started overflowing with pieces for sale and pieces waiting to be brought into salable condition, I looked for a place to rent in a high-traffic area. I found a small space on the south side of town, and moved my merchandise in with Sammy's help.

But stuff still accumulated in my garage. Some of it I took to other dealers, and things I wanted to keep I showed to several dealers to determine what they were worth. After a while I got to know all the major dealers in northeast Ohio. I developed a knack for wheeling and dealing, and I got to know which dealers I could trust. Not all were honest. One dealer who was also an auctioneer I gave about $2500 worth of items to auction off. I expected to net about $1500. Instead, I received a check for $230 from him. I resolved never to put stuff up for auction again. Now dealers that know me say, "That Marty, she's got a good eye for antiques."

In order that Sammy and I could be together, I decided to get another place to stay. He and I rented an apartment in the north part of town, agreeing to split the rent. So then I was living in two places, telling Frank I was working nights, and feeling guilty about having to lie to him. I had to keep Sammy away from Frank. Each one was a Taurus - in other words, both were stubborn bulls. Sammy acted as though he understood completely that I couldn't bear to hurt Frank by telling him I had another boyfriend. We agreed to continue being together at the apartment. I was so happy whenever I was with Sammy. I hoped fervently that it would work out, that I could have both a white man and a black man, and that all of us could live this way happily ever after.

It worked for less than a year, this mixed-up, merry-go-round kind of life I was leading. Sammy did little repair jobs around my house while Frank was away. Then I would have to come up with an explanation.

"Who fixed the porch door?" Frank wanted to know.

"Oh, I hired a man to do it, because I knew you were too busy."

At times I took Corky with me to the apartment I shared with Sammy. But after a while, he'd be itching to go home.

"I wanna go home, I wanna go to Frank," he pleaded.

This did not sit well with Sammy. I suppose he wondered why Corky should prefer being with Frank rather than with him. But that didn't seem to me a good reason to start drinking. Frequently he showed up at the apartment with liquor on his breath. He became surly and uncooperative. Then he stopped paying his share of the apartment rent.

One evening I heard a sound from the bedroom, and asked Sammy, "What was that?"

"Oh, my brother's got some girl in there."

Next thing I knew, his brother brought his belongings to our apartment and wouldn't leave. So now we had a permanent house guest. Groups of rowdy men, friends of Sammy's brother, started congregating at the apartment, leaving piles of empty beer bottles when they left. When I asked Sammy to get his brother out, he told me in a most forceful, insolent manner, "Wherever I'm at, my brother comes with me." I watched my apartment, my secret hangout in which to spend time with the man I loved, turn into a neighborhood clubhouse.

I didn't want Corky exposed to the kind of behavior we were unwillingly witnessing. He had sense enough to realize that something was wrong.

"Momma, I don' wanna be around that beer-drinkin' Sammy," he'd say. "I wanna go home."

Sammy turned into a full-blown alcoholic. I gave up the apartment, relieved, yet regretful that my plans had proved unworkable. From then on, I could see that Sammy was changing from a calm talented Dr. Jekyll into a demented Mr. Hyde. From a funny, charming fellow, he turned into a possessive, demanding degenerate. I suspected that he was into drugs, although I had no proof. It became impossible to have a decent conversation with him any more, and I resented not being able to express myself when with him. I couldn't tell Frank what was bothering me, and so my feelings stewed inside, ready to bubble over with volcanic fury.

In the past I had often taken Corky to the Putt-Putt Golf, and when I saw he had developed a keen love of golfing, I bought him a set of Spalding golf clubs that took me a year and a half to pay for. He used them at the city-owned golf course, and he loved to watch golf matches on TV.

One day Corky's golf clubs disappeared from the apartment. I asked Sammy about them. He denied knowing anything about their whereabouts. But I knew darn well that Sammy had taken them and sold them to get drug money. I immediately took my fur jackets and good jewelry to my mother's house.

Corky's quarters and dimes, which he had saved lovingly, disappeared also. When I confronted Sammy, all he would say was, "You give Corky too much anyway." It was evident he resented Corky, even though outwardly he pretended to like him.

I knew many antique dealers and pawnshop owners by this time, so whenever I found something of mine missing, I made the rounds of dealers in an attempt to locate the item. I retrieved several pieces of my jewelry in this way.

Whereas Sammy had at first helped me in my antique store, now, as his personality disintegrated, he made a cock-eyed rule that I was only allowed in "our" store at certain times. I found that merchandise was disappearing. Nickels, dimes, quarters, even pennies vanished from the cash box. I found that I had to hide my money so that I could pay rent for the store. Then the TV and the microwave that I kept in the back room disappeared. One day I came home and discovered the piano was gone. Sammy had sold it, right out of my house, to get money for drugs.

Occasionally, while at my house, Sammy said to me, "I'm goin' down to fix the hot water tank. Somethin's wrong with the hot water."

The tank finally developed a hole as big as a dime, and had to be replaced. Under the old tank, I found a cocaine pipe. Sammy had been going down to the basement to smoke a hit of cocaine.

It was no use saying anything to him. My words never registered on his clouded brain. Like any addict, his mind only concentrated on when and where he could get his next hit.

By this time, Frank was aware of Sammy. He understood black domestic problems and ignored them, feeling there was nothing he could do.

Sammy, on his part, resented Frank, just like Marlon had done. Once I caught him underneath Frank's truck, which was parked in my driveway. He emerged, holding a large knife, which he tried to hide behind his back when he saw me. He didn't speak, but walked quickly to the back yard and disappeared. He had just cut Frank's gas line, and gasoline was streaming down the driveway into the gutter.

I knew I had to get rid of Sammy.

If any other man would have become the least bit interested in me during this time, that man would have immediately backed off upon realizing I was involved with a crack addict. I knew I'd have to forget about having a black man in my life. In the meantime, Frank was sticking like glue, hanging in with me and Corky, no matter what. He was not living with us anymore, but would drop in several times a week. If we were not home, he left little gifts for me or Corky on the kitchen counter. It might be an attractive cup and saucer that he found at a garage sale, or a pot pie for Corky, or a ten-dollar bill for him. I appreciated Frank's attentiveness, but I was miserable, not knowing what to do about Sammy.

Chapter 20

For many years I had known that Corky's ears were very sensitive. Some sounds seemed to bother him greatly, while others not at all. Although over the years his discomfort had lessened, I wondered, could there be a way to protect his ears from this?

In a health food store, I happened to pick up a brochure that described a procedure called Auditory Desensitization. I discovered a hearing clinic in Cincinnati that offered the procedure, so I made an appointment for Corky.

Auditory Desensitization Training is a hearing enhancement process developed by Dr. Guy Berard, a French ear, nose and throat doctor. In recent years it has been applied with some success to autistic individuals.

Dr. Berard, when a young man, found himself growing deaf. He treated himself by playing music that contained frequencies he was having trouble hearing. He found that his ears adjusted, or compensated, and grew more acute at those frequencies. He believed that an individual's hearing is flexible; it can be adjusted up or down. People living near railroad tracks don't pay attention to a train whistle or the rumbling along the tracks, and people living near a firehouse soon learn to ignore the sound of a siren. Therefore, Dr. Berard reasoned, perhaps autistic children can be trained to ignore frequencies that bother them, and conversely, they could be trained to become more attuned to those frequencies they hardly hear at all.

He began to treat children with hearing difficulties, especially children whose hearing is hyper, that is, they hear too well and certain sounds are painful to them. Such children think everyone hears sounds the same way they do, and since other people don't seem to be bothered at all, they conclude they are abnormal, even crazy. When their hearing is adjusted, they experience an enormous sense of relief. Often their other senses become more normal also.

The training consists of half-hour sessions performed twice a day, for ten consecutive days, with equipment designed just for that purpose. The tester first determines the tolerance level or threshold of discomfort of the subject, using tones of various frequencies. Starting at a level of about 20 decibels below the threshold of discomfort, the sound is gradually increased. Also the time limit at each level is slowly increased, up to about fifteen minutes. Besides single tones, white noise and music can also be presented.

The process reduces the patient's tendency to block out annoying sounds, and lessens the sensitivity to these sounds. Thus the perception of all incoming auditory information is improved, as well as the ability to understand what is said.

Psychologists Dr. Bernard Rimland and Dr. Stephen Edelson used the technique on autistic children and reported improved ability to understand what is said to them, improved articulation and memory for routine information, and reduced irritability, self-stimulating behaviors, restlessness, distractability, and repeating what is said to them.

Cincinnati was one of the first cities in the U.S. to carry out clinical trials of this program. I had been told that the program works well for some autistic individuals and less well in others. But I felt it was worth a try.

Corky and I were in Cincinnati for two weeks. The doctor showed both of us the soundproof booth, earphones, and amplifier for modifying sound. He adjusted the dials and found the frequencies that Corky found unpleasant. He showed me the graphs that the machine drew. The peaks showed where Corky had hyper hearing, and the valleys, where it was hypo. After several days, the line on the graphs became more undulating. There were no more sharp peaks, only rounded hills and shallow valleys.

The entire treatment cost me $1200. I'm not sure whether it helped Corky a whole lot. His sensitivity to sounds did improve, but his behavior had progressed all along as a result of my patiently working with him.

I had a T-shirt made for Corky with the words "I Survived Auditory Training" emblazoned on the back, which he wore to his classes at Weaver. I felt it might gain him Brownie points at school, and show that his mother is going all out for him. One of the Weaver staff got interested enough to ask me questions about the procedure.

In recent days I read a book titled "The Sound of a Miracle" by Annabel Stehli, in which she tells how auditory training turned around her autistic daughter's life at age eleven. Georgiana could hear the blood coursing through her body; her own breathing sounded like a

MY EVALUATION OF CORKY'S BEHAVIOR AFTER AUDITORY DESENSITIZATION

	Not at all A problem	Problem Mild	Problem Moderate	Problem Severe
1. Excessively active at home			X	
2. Injures self			X	
3. Listless, sluggish, inactive	X			
4. Aggressive to others	X			
5. Seeks isolation from others		X		
6. Meaningless recurring body movements			X	
7. Boisterous (inappropriately noisy and rough	X			
8. Screams inappropriately	X			
9. Talks excessively				X
10. Temper tantrums		X		
11. Stereotyped repetitive movements			X	
12. Preoccupied, stares into space		X		
13. Impulsive (acts without thinking)			X	
14. Irritable & whiny			X	
15. Restless, unable to sit still		X		
16. Withdrawn; prefers solitary activities		X		
17. Odd, bizarre in behavior		X		
18. Disobedient, difficult to control			X	
19. Yells at inappropriate times		X		
20. Fixed facial expression; lacks emotional reactivity		X		
21. Disturbs others		X		
22. Repetitive speech				X
23. Does nothing but sit and watch others	X			
24. Uncooperative			X	

25. Depressed mood		X	
26. Resists any form of physical contact			X
27. Moves or rolls head back & forth		X	
28. Does not pay attention to instructions		X	
29. Demands must be met immediately		X	
30. Isolates himself from peers		X	
31. Disrupts group activities	X		
32. Sits or stands in one position for a long time		X	
33. Talks to self loudly				X
34. Cries over minor annoyances and hurts			X
Repetitive hand, body or head movements			X
36. Mood changes quickly			X
37. Unresponsive to school activities			X
38. Does not stay in seat during lesson period		X	
39. Will not sit still for any length of time		X	
40. Is difficult to reach or contact		X	
41. Cries or screams inappropriately		X	
42. Prefers to be alone			X
43. Does not try to communicate by words or gestures	X		
44. Easily distractible		X	
45. Waves or shakes the extremities repeatedly		X	
46. Repeats a word or phrase over and over				X
47. Stamps foot while banging objects or slamming doors	X		
48. Constantly runs or jumps around the room		X	
49. Rocks body back & forth		X	

50. Deliberately hurts self				X
51. Pays no attention when spoken to			X	
52. Does physical violence to self			X	
53. Inactive, never moves spontaneously		X		
54. Tends to be excessively active	X			
55. Responds negatively to affection			X	
56. Deliberately ignores directions		X		
57. Throws temper tantrums when he does not get own way		X		
58. Shows few social reaction to others			X	
59. Does not pay attention to instructions 50% or more of time			X	
60. Does not listen carefully to directions, often necessary to repeat instructions				X
61. Says "Huh?" and "What?" at least 5 or more times a day	X			
62. Cannot attend to auditory stimuli for more than a few seconds		X		
63. Short attention span			X	
64. Daydreams, attention drifts		X		
65. Easily distracted by background sounds			X	
66. Difficulty with phonics			X	
67. Problems with sound discrimination		X		
68. Trouble recalling a sequence he has heard		X		
69. Forgets what is said in a few minutes		X		
70. Does not remember simple routine things from day to day		X		
71. Problems recalling what was heard last week, month, year	X			
72. Difficulty following auditory directions			X	
73. Often misunderstands what is said			X	

74. Does not comprehend many words-verbal concepts for age/grade level	X	
75. Slow or delayed response to verbal stimuli	X	
76. Has a language problem (morphology, syntax, vocabulary, phonology)	X	
77. Has an articulation (phonology) problem	X	
78. Cannot always relate what is heard with what is seen	X	
79. Learns poorly through the auditory channel	X	
80. Lacks motivation to learn	X	
81. Performance is below average in one or more subject areas		X

From ABC Checklist

windstorm, and an ordinary rainfall sounded like a tidal wave to her. The author underwent terrible guilt feelings that were reinforced by various doctors and psychologists, who told her Georgie's problems were caused by a cold, rejecting mother. Annabel knew that wasn't true; her deep love for her daughter showed on every page of her book. Of course, that theory of autism was long ago rejected by psychologists.

To compound Annabel's problems, her older daughter suffered from leukemia and eventually died, and her husband walked out on her. I cried as I read her story. How could one person cope with so much misery? I was overjoyed upon reading that she married another man, very understanding and sensitive, and that Georgie's problems were largely resolved through the auditory training program. Since Georgie's miraculous recovery, her parents have founded the Georgiana Foundation to disseminate information on auditory training and to teach the technique.

In May 1993, when Corky was close to twenty-two years old, it was time for his graduation from Weaver School. I told my various family members about the upcoming ceremony, but I had no illusions about their attendance. I was simply curious whether any of them would bother to attend.

I had developed another deep friendship at that time. Robert Robey was a short white man who had ventured quite by chance into my antique store one day. After some conversation and several more visits, we developed a deep rapport. Robert was greatly interested in Corky because he also was born with a handicap. It was a condition called Moebius syndrome, and is a failure of two nerves in the head to develop properly before birth. The result is an inability to smile, a somewhat slurred speech, and delayed muscle development. In me Robert saw images of his mother, who had worked with him to develop his leg muscles in the years he had to wear leg braces, and had encouraged him throughout his childhood. In Corky, Robert saw a reflection of himself, not quite rising above his handicap, but making the most of his abilities in spite of it.

Having become my close friend, Robert was a logical person to invite to Corky's graduation. Frank was not available because he had to work.

111

Corky took his place among the eight graduating students as they filed into the hall, resplendent in royal blue caps and gowns, while the Weaver handbell choir rang out the notes of Beethoven's "Ode to Joy". The entire student body seemed to be present, except for the very youngest. Several immobile students came in seated in their wheelchairs.

Corky had been chosen to give the graduation speech, which someone on the faculty had written for him to read. It was all about growth and accomplishment. I felt he read it very well.

Listening to him, tears welled up in my eyes. I thought of how far he had come since that far-off day I had first enrolled him. I thought of all he had been through at Weaver, the many times he had rushed from the van into the house, so frustrated and teary-eyed, and I would have to calm him down and comfort him. I remembered the leather jacket that was ruined, and the girl student who used to pick on him relentlessly. All this had taken seventeen years, and the graduation ceremony was the culmination.

I turned to Robert and asked him, "Do you think he realizes now that he's somebody?" Robert told me later that the event was a most moving experience for him.

Several special awards were given out. One - a gold plaque - went to Corky as "most improved student."

True to form, none of my family showed up for the ceremony. Of all the relatives, only Corky's Aunt Beverly came.

At the close of the ceremony, the folding chairs were removed from the hall, or placed along the walls, to make way for the prom, which followed immediately after. The students removed their caps and gowns to reveal formal white dinner jackets and long gowns. I had arranged to have Corky's cousin Cordella be his date for the prom. I also arranged for a limousine to bring them home later.

A DJ started playing dance music, and couples drifted onto the dance floor.

Then came an announcement: the King of the Prom is...Corky Diamond! He went up to receive his crown, a big smile creasing his face. He returned to his seat with a slight swagger in his walk, his chest out, his beaming facial expression all indicating "I'm the man of the hour!"

112

For the rest of the evening, girls lined up to dance with Corky, whether it was disco, line dancing, or slow dreamy numbers. Every girl in the hall, it seemed, had to dance at least once with the King.

Cordella had been reluctant to come. I had found it necessary to bribe her with promises of a new dress for the evening, new shoes, earrings, and purse. I also purchased the carnation corsage that she wore. She was not used to being around handicapped people, and seemed uncomfortable being surrounded by so many. But after Corky's crowning she relaxed and began to enjoy herself.

The wheelchair-bound students did not let their immobility stop them from participating. They rolled back and forth, spun their chairs around, and waved their arms in time to the music. It was uplifting to watch them enjoy themselves.

Again I remembered that Corky had had a lot of rough days at Weaver, probably more of those than easy days. Perhaps the school staff realized that, and now tried to make up for all the distress they caused by making him King of the Prom. I cried and rejoiced at the same time.

My friend Robert videotaped the entire evening, while I wandered through the hall, occasionally stopping to pat Corky on the back and ask, "You havin' fun?" to which he replied with an emphatic "Yeah!"

I showed the video to my mother when I next visited her. She felt sorry that she hadn't come to witness our triumph and Corky's moment in the sun.

Each of us has different talents,
different dreams, different
destinations.
But we all have the power
to make a new tomorrow.
In pride,
Weaver School Graduates and Faculty
announce their Achievement Ceremony
Friday, May twenty-first
Nineteen hundred and ninety-three
at seven-thirty in the evening
Weaver School
Tallmadge, Ohio

Invitation to
Corky's graduation

Chapter 21

The situation between Sammy and me continued to deteriorate.

Sammy initiated tactics with me that I call the Auto Parts Con Game. About twice a week I would get in my car to drive to my store, and my car wouldn't start. I would go back into the house, disgusted and upset, make a cup of coffee, perhaps smoke a cigarette, and ponder what to do. Before long, Sammy would show up.

"What's wrong with your car now?" he would ask. "Let me take a look at it."

He opened up the hood, fiddled around with wires or cables, and told me, "Now try it."

When it started, he would grin and bask in my expressions of thanks.

Sometimes he said, "You need a new part. Let me go to Auto Zone and get it for you. Give me a dollar so I can take the bus down."

I handed him a dollar bill, or, if I had no change, a five or a ten. He never seemed to get any change at Auto Zone for whatever part he purchased. And he never showed me a receipt from the store.

One day Sammy and I stopped at a gas station in my car. A black couple stood beside a Mercedes-Benz, arguing vociferously. The woman, still angry, marched into the service station. While she was inside, the man opened the hood of the Mercedes and yanked out a few wires. I watched, dumbfounded, then looked at Sammy with sudden comprehension.

"So that's how it's done!" I said.

"You don't know what you talkin' about!"

But I knew. I realized I was being continually sabotaged.

There are four kinds of black men: those with steady jobs, those who do odd jobs, those who have no jobs, and those who hustle, meaning they beg, steal, or scrounge for whatever they can get from others. A man who does not have a steady job will hook up with a woman who is employed and owns a car.

At night he disconnects something in her car. Consequently it won't start when she has to leave for work the next morning. She takes the bus instead. He fixes the car and uses it the rest of the day, cruising around with his buddies, drinking beer, smoking pot, or

115

getting high on cocaine. Even if the man holds a job, or claims to hold a job, he will pretend to be the knight in shining armor coming to the rescue. At great sacrifice he offers to go AWOL from the alleged job in order to get the car running. He secretly hopes the woman will take a bus, or otherwise leave the scene so that he can indulge himself the rest of the day.

It's a pitiful situation, but I knew it was very widespread. The woman gets to progressively depend on her man for keeping her car running. He comes out looking like a hero for fixing the car, and he gets to do whatever he wants on those days that he has wheels.

That was how Sammy manipulated me, over a four-year period and several different cars. He played on my ignorance of auto mechanics to make himself indispensable to me. Even if he did occasionally show me a receipt for $25 or $40 for a car part, how did I know he hadn't picked it up off the floor at Auto Zone, or previously obtained it from a friend? I finally put a stop to his game, but it was at great inconvenience to myself: I refused to buy another car when the last one gave out. From then on, I walked, rode the bus, or bummed rides from others.

Perhaps in my next reincarnation, I'll make it a point to learn auto mechanics.

I asked Sammy to stay away from me. "Just go, I don't wanna see you around no more, especially not here in my house."

He laughed. "I ain't goin' nowhere. I'm never gonna leave you."

So I joined the legions of African-American women who are caught in the cocaine-alcohol trap set up by an African-American man who abuses and victimizes the woman - or else induces the woman to become a user too. Like a fly caught in a spider web, there is no escape from a man like that. You just gotta take it, baby.

How could I keep Sammy away from my house? He found ways to get in, whether I was home or not. I went to court to get a restraining order for him to stop harassing me. He ignored the court order.

Then he started sleeping in his car across the street from my house. In the middle of the night he came and knocked at my window. If I didn't do something, he would wake Corky, and also Frank, if it was one of the nights Frank spent with us. I felt protective towards both of them, and I didn't want my problem to become their problem too. I got up and pacified Sammy sexually to get rid of him, at least for that night.

Over a three-year period, I must have called the police two hundred times to complain that Sammy was harassing me. The policemen wrote up their report and promised to watch the house, but nothing ever changed. Black on black domestic violence did not interest the cops as long as there was no bloodshed. My calling the police didn't faze Sammy at all.

"Tell me you love me," Sammy would say in his best whipped-cream voice.

"No, I don't love you, and I want you to leave me alone!" Why was he so obsessed with me?

One day, Sammy ended up in jail, after being arrested on a drug charge. So now I was rid of him - at least for a year.

"Sammy blew it," Corky commented. "He can't go to a movie. Can't go to a restaurant..." And can't be bothering me, I added silently.

The only good thing that came out of my involvement with Sammy was that it taught Corky there are good people and bad people. Sometimes Corky discovered me crying softly.

"Momma, why you cryin'?" he asked. "That Sammy not here today."

I knew Corky would protect me if I were ever physically attacked. More than once Corky declared, "If Sammy hurts my Momma, I'm gonna hit him with a baseball bat and call the police."

I was a small measure of comfort for me.

Chapter 22

(by Erica)

I had been looking forward to meeting Corky for about six months.

On a sunny September morning, I arrived at Marty's house, a blue and white Cape Cod on a busy thoroughfare that is mostly residential but also has several churches. The front yard is shaded by two pin oaks and two pine trees. A wooden fence separates it from the street and the neighboring lots. Marty motioned me to a lawn chair near the front door, while she seated herself on a two-seat bench.

We had originally arranged to meet at a nearby fast-food restaurant, but then she remembered she had placed an ad for a yard sale, so she couldn't leave the house. While we talked, people drove up and looked at the merchandise arrayed along the fence, mostly furniture items. But nobody bought anything. Undiscouraged, Marty told me she expected to take in about three hundred dollars by evening.

"It's Friday, people have their paychecks, they'll buy something."

She showed me two chairs whose seats Sammy had recovered with white damask-like material. He had sprayed the backs and legs with gold paint.

"Don't they look nice?" she asked. "I think they'll sell."

She herself was working on a dried flower arrangement, stalks of teasel and green leaves laid out artistically on a gold picture frame. As I watched, she added three stalks of wheat, then surveyed the result with satisfaction. She had sold similar pieces at arts and crafts shows.

"I had thirty pieces like this at my last show, and I sold them all. Anywhere from twelve to fifty dollars. I think I'll ask fifteen for this one."

Hearing Corky stir inside, she called him to come out. A strapping young man, a little on the hefty side, opened the door but remained in the doorway as his mother introduced us. I wanted to shake his hand, but it was on the door, holding it open.

"Won't you come out?" Marty asked.

"Mat is wet," he said. He was shoeless, only white socks on his feet. He disappeared inside and emerged a moment later with sneakers on, and sat down beside his mother. She rumpled his close-cropped hair affectionately.

"He just took a shower. He takes good care of himself. He's got a whole ritual involving brushing his teeth. Show Erica your teeth."

He opened his mouth, revealing a perfect set of white teeth.

"I hear you like to swim," I said to Corky. "Where do you go swimming?"

"Natatorium."

Marty mentioned several Akron pools open to the public.

"Show me how you swim. Is it like this?" I asked, making crawl motions with my arms. He made similar motions, opening and closing his mouth to simulate breathing.

"He swims like a dolphin. He has a style all his own," Marty said proudly.

"Erica Stux has a belt," Corky remarked. Evidently his mother had made him learn my name, and he was eager to use it. He had a wide leather belt holding up his jeans, and must have compared mine to his. The way he spat out his words reminded me of the speech and mannerisms of Dustin Hoffman in the movie "Rain Man."

"Do you like animals?" I asked, remembering that I'd read autistic individuals seem to have some rapport with them.

"I like animals."

"What kind do you like? Dogs, cats?"

"All of 'em."

Our conversation turned to Corky's favorite TV shows, one of which is reruns of the Statler Brothers.

"What time are they on?" Marty asked him.

"Saturday, nine o'clock."

Marty turned to me. "He memorizes the TV Guide. He has a photographic memory."

"Barbara Mandrell and the Mandrell Sisters!" Corky declaimed dramatically, imitating the announcer of another favorite show.

"Corky, if I had a twenty dollar bill with an S on it, where would it come from?" his mother asked.

"Cleveland." he said, without hesitation.

119

"If I had a twenty dollar bill with an M on it, where would it come from?"

"St. Louis."

"See, he knows things no one else would know," she said with evident pride.

Marty explained to me that ever since Corky's graduation from Weaver School, he has been under the jurisdiction of the Board of Vocational Rehabilitation. The two of them meet with the BVR staff every six weeks or so. Upon hearing his mother mention the name of one staff member, Corky remarked, "She's got big legs, big bum, big tiddies."

"That's not nice," his mother admonished him, "to talk about someone's bum or tiddies."

When a customer for the yard sale pulled up, Corky disappeared into the house. After the customer left, I asked Marty, "Will he talk to anyone, or just people he knows?"

"He's friendly, but I'm trying to teach him there are good people and bad people."

"What makes a person bad?"

"Oh, people that ask too many favors of you, or are always asking to borrow something from you...or are drug users." She mentioned a woman's name, raising her voice so that Corky could hear inside. "Is she a good person or a bad person?"

"Bad person."

Marty was on her second cigarette since I arrived.

"What about your smoking? Does Corky smoke?"

"No, he hates it. He hides my ashtrays. Usually I don't smoke in the house, though."

It figures. Autistics are either overly sensitive to loud noises, strong odors, or forceful touching, or else they seek out such stimulants. Corky evidently belonged to the first group, at least with regard to smell.

Marty persuaded me to have a cup of tea with her. While she disappeared to prepare it. Corky came to the door.

"Ma'am, would you like sugar or honey in your tea?"

"A little honey, please." I was pleasantly surprised at his polite manner.

After we finished our tea, Marty invited me into the house. Corky was napping on the living room floor. A game show was in progress on the TV. Eleven medals and a number of ribbons - Corky's swimming awards - hung on the living room wall. Dominating the room was a framed blow-up of Marty's newspaper article from Las Vegas. Various photos of Corky at different ages were arranged on the walls. It was evident to me that Marty was doing her best to make Corky feel important.

I hoped he would consider me a "good person."

Chapter 23

(by Erica)

About a month had passed since my first meeting with Corky. I needed to see Marty again, so I dialed her number. After four rings, a man's voice said "Hello!"

"Is Marty there?" I asked, not sure to whom I was speaking.

"Momma? She's in Hartville today, to make some money."

I knew that she sometimes took merchandise to sell at the Hartville flea market, about twenty miles from Akron.

"Corky, this is Erica. Remember me?"

"Yep."

"So she's in Hartville today? Will you tell her I called?"

There was a click; he's already hung up by the time I finished the question. But I was pleased to find out he can answer the phone and carry on a rudimentary conversation.

A month later, I needed to call again.

"Corky, is your momma there?"

"I wait till Momma comes back."

"Do you know when she'll be home?"

"I wait till Momma comes back. Who's this?"

"Erica. Remember me?"

"Yep."

"Okay, tell her I need to see her again."

"Okay, bye."

"Thank you, Corky. Bye."

Corky was at that time working mornings at the Goodwill building. He had had various part-time jobs since he was eighteen, the first one being a federally-funded summer program for disadvantaged youth, which placed him as a landscaping assistant. The guidance counselor in charge of this program was wonderful to Corky, the first black man to ever give him solicitous attention, according to Marty.

Then Weaver School put him in its work-study program. He was given a dishwashing job at a church, twenty hours a week. After that came custodial work, and then a car-washing job.

122

Corky did well at the carwash. His size was an asset, allowing him to reach easily across the top of the cars. Sometimes he worked too fast and missed a spot, but on the whole, his work was considered satisfactory. There were minor disturbances when Corky would nurse a grudge or stew about an incident all day, bursting into loud exclamations both at work and on the van taking him home. Other times he disturbed his coworkers by reciting TV commercials.

Corky's job was broken down into individual steps, which he could review any time. His supervisor wrote a comment on an evaluation sheet for each day, such as "Very good day, did 12 cars" or "Didn't listen well today, but work was still good."

Shortly before Corky's graduation, he underwent a vocational appraisal. The evaluator's recommendation was that he needed to develop living skills and be encouraged to initiate work tasks. This surprised Marty; living skills was something she had inculcated in him for years already through her persistent teaching. The appraisal stated that Corky would probably require a job coach all his life.

Since his graduation, Corky was under the jurisdiction of the Bureau of Vocational Rehabilitation. In 1995, he was doing janitorial work three hours each morning at the Goodwill building near downtown Akron. His job included sweeping the stairwells of the six-floor building and carrying supplies upstairs. Sometimes he was picked up by a van, and sometimes he took the city bus downtown. Later in the day, the city bus took him within a block of his home. He knew which bus to take, but sometimes he would forget to get off, lulled, perhaps, by the purr of the motor. There were times when the driver would drive his entire route two or three times, and Corky would still be aboard. Marty finally told the drivers where they should have Corky get off.

The following rules are to be reviewed with Corky each morning upon arrival to school. Each time Corky violates a rule, staff are to ask Corky which rule he violated and have him to repeat the rule. Each rule violation is recorded on the data sheet.

<u>Rules</u>

1. Follow Directions
2. Stay within assigned area and ask permission when leaving.
3. Speak politely to others. (No insults, rude or degrading statements, interruptions, or bossing).
4. Do not repeat self unless asked to do so. No talking to self.

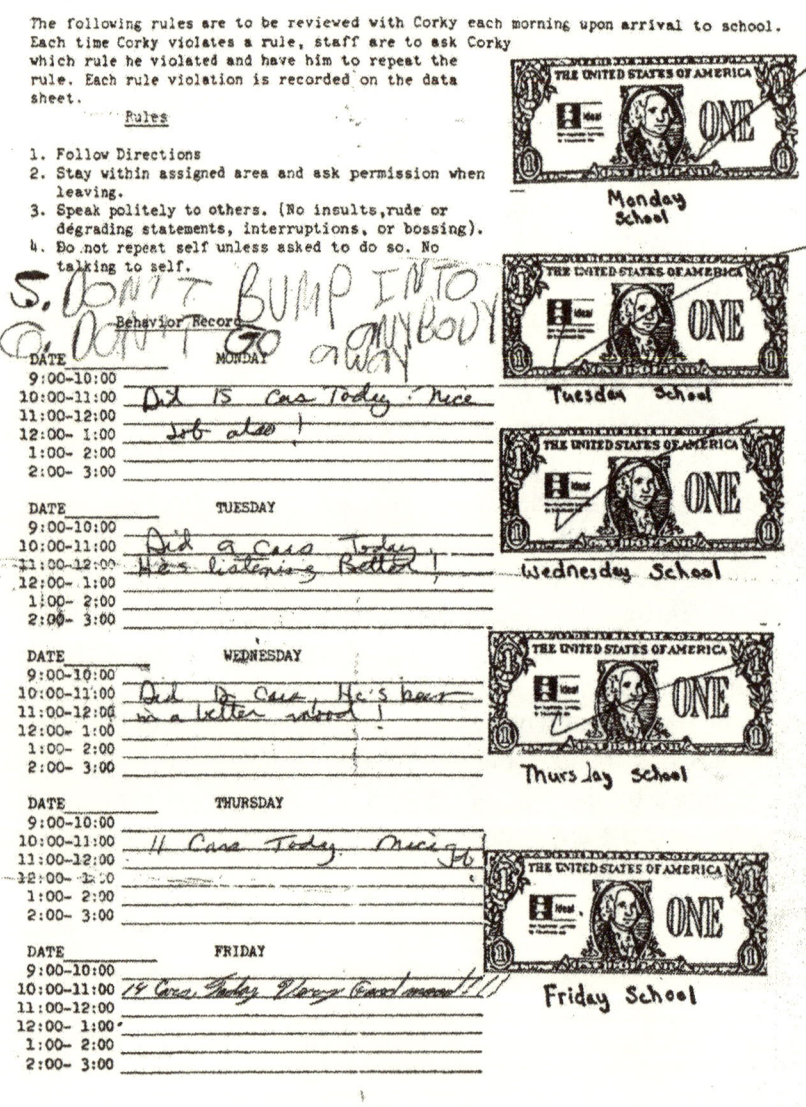

5. DON'T BUMP INTO ANYBODY
DON'T GO AWAY

Behavior Record

DATE	MONDAY
9:00-10:00	
10:00-11:00	Did 15 Cars Today. Nice
11:00-12:00	Job also!
12:00- 1:00	
1:00- 2:00	
2:00- 3:00	

Monday School

DATE	TUESDAY
9:00-10:00	
10:00-11:00	Did 9 Cars Today
11:00-12:00	His listening Better!
12:00- 1:00	
1:00- 2:00	
2:00- 3:00	

Tuesday School

Wednesday School

DATE	WEDNESDAY
9:00-10:00	
10:00-11:00	Did 10 Cars, He's been
11:00-12:00	in a better mood!
12:00- 1:00	
1:00- 2:00	
2:00- 3:00	

Thursday School

DATE	THURSDAY
9:00-10:00	
10:00-11:00	11 Cars Today. Nice Job
11:00-12:00	
12:00- 1:00	
1:00- 2:00	
2:00- 3:00	

DATE	FRIDAY
9:00-10:00	
10:00-11:00	14 Cars Today. Very Good mood!!!
11:00-12:00	
12:00- 1:00	
1:00- 2:00	
2:00- 3:00	

Friday School

The following rules are to be reviewed with Corky each morning upon arrival to school. Each time Corky violates a rule, staff are to ask Corky which rule he violated and have him to repeat the rule. Each rule violation is recorded on the data sheet.

Rules

1. Follow Directions
2. Stay within assigned area and ask permission when leaving.
3. Speak politely to others. (No insults, rude or degrading statements, interruptions, or bossing).
4. Do not repeat self unless asked to do so. No talking to self.

Monday
School

Behavior Record

DATE 3-22-93   MONDAY
9:00-10:00 |||
10:00-11:00
11:00-12:00 |||
12:00- 1:00 ||
1:00- 2:00
2:00- 3:00

Tuesday   School

DATE 3-23-93   TUESDAY
9:00-10:00   9 Curs
10:00-11:00   good Job Today Good Mood
11:00-12:00
12:00- 1:00
1:00- 2:00
2:00- 3:00

Wednesday School

DATE_____   WEDNESDAY
9:00-10:00   13 Cars
10:00-11:00
11:00-12:00   Good Job Today
12:00- 1:00
1:00- 2:00
2:00- 3:00

Thursday School

DATE_____   THURSDAY
9:00-10:00   16 Curs Today. He was
10:00-11:00   upset this morning. Had to
11:00-12:00   give aspirin + extra Break
12:00- 1:00   but was okay.
1:00- 2:00
2:00- 3:00

DATE_____   FRIDAY
9:00-10:00
10:00-11:00   15 cars, a little
11:00-12:00   stubborn, but got calmed
12:00- 1:00   down
1:00- 2:00
2:00- 3:00

Friday School

The **Reading Free Vocational Interest Inventory-Revised** was completed.
Norms used: Adult handicapped worker norms

HIGH INTEREST   **LOW INTEREST**

Food service   Horticulture
Personal service   Housekeeping
Laundry service
Materials handling

VOCATIONAL APPRAISAL - Corky Diamond

The student's general intellectual skills were assessed with the __Leiter International Performance Scale__

APS ASSESSMENT DATE: January 23, 1991

　　　M.A. score 4 yrs. 8 months　　　　I.Q. 36

Academic achievement was assessed with: __Wide Range Achievement Test-Revised (1-29-91)__
　　　Reading　　　SS 59　　　Age equivalent <3
　　　Spelling　　　SS 55　　　Age equivalent <3
　　　Arithmetic　　SS <46　　Age equivalent <3

The **McCarron-Dial Work Evaluation System** was completed

Subtest	Standard Score	Vocational Placement
M.A.N.D. (motor)		
Fine Motor	57	Low extended/prevocational
Gross Motor	59	Low extended/prevocational
Total Motor	58	Low extended/prevocational
Haptic (sensory integration) right	29	Basic skills
B.V.M.G.T. (visual motor)	55	Low extended/prevocational
S.S.S.Q. (functional skills)	51	Low extended/prevocational
O.E.I. (emotional rating)	39	Work activities
B.R.S. (behavioral rating)	55	Low extended/prevocational
Verbal cognitive/spatial	IQ 32	Basic skills
Peabody picture vocabulary	<40	Prevocational training

Prevocational Skills

According to the computerized trait analysis from the McCarron Dial System, Corky's average factor standard score, for those factors measured, is 45.6. The score is associated with the program level of work activity/prevocational training. Scores falling above his overall average factor standard score include his visual motor skills, fine, gross, and total motor skills, emotional and behavioral ratings, and functional living skills. Scores falling below his average factor standard score include his cognitive ability, verbal receptivity, and visual tactile skills.

The MAND reviews the motor characteristic of persistence control, muscle power, kinesthetic integration, and bimanual dexterity. Corky's scores were compared to the adult neuropsychologically disabled norm group. Compared to this norm group, his motor skills are fairly well developed at a 95-115 standard score range. He has the most skill in bimanual dexterity with a standard score of 115, kinesthetic integration was 110, and persistence control muscle power was at 95. Compared to this norm group, Corky's motor skills are very well developed. Compared to non-disabled peers, Corky's motor skills are within the second standard deviation range below normal.

The STREET SURVIVAL SKILLS QUESTIONNAIRE was completed to assess Corky's independent living or functional skills. Corky identified all basic colors. He had difficulty matching color shades. Corky identified the concepts of up and down and right, but had difficulty with left, through, between, top, most, same, inside, middle, and front. Corky is very knowledgeable of functional signs. He identified all signs except exit, do not disturb, and flammable. These signs involved reading rather than universal symbols. Corky is somewhat familiar with basic household tools. He identified a saw, wire pliers, crow bar, stapler, drill, level, hammer, and hack saw. He had difficulty with electric tools such as a jig saw and electric saw. He also had difficulty with identifying the correct tool with the various situation. Corky identified basic kitchen utensils and the proper food storage for refrigeration and freezing. Corky also identified which foods need to be cooked and which foods can be eaten raw. He had difficulty with stove and oven dial selections. Corky is familiar where to measure for clothing sizes. He is also familiar with cleaning and laundry supplies but not familiar with washer and dryer dial settings. Corky is familiar with personal grooming products. He identified what to use for a burn and eye contamination but not a severe cut. He is able to identify a thermometer, temperature which indicates the need for immediate medical care, how to clean a thermometer, and what to use to lower a fever. Corky had difficulty with understanding a prescription drug label even when it was read to him. He also is not familiar with reflective clothing to be worn at night time, and how to deal with a drowning situation. He is familiar with correct lifting procedures, what to use for eye protection, and aerosol can safety. Corky had difficulty identifying how to hold his hands when cutting with a knife and how to deal with a grease fire. Corky is familiar with public services located at a bank, post office, and drug store. He identified you purchase stamps at a post office but had difficulty knowing where to put the stamp on the envelope. Corky identified the "local" slot at a post office. He identified a paycheck. He did have difficulty with identifying deposit form information and a correctly written check. Corky is familiar with how to dial the operator on a push button and rotary phone and can dial a number when given a number for visual matching. He knew to look up a person's last name in the telephone directory but had difficulty pursuing that idea. Corky can tell time to the minute on an analog or digital clock. Manipulating time amounts is difficult for Corky. He can identify days of the week and the months of the year in the correct order but had difficulty reading a calendar. Corky identified all coins, bills, and some coin associations. He had difficulty adding coins and making change. Corky identified the hottest and coldest temperatures on a thermometer but could not associate a temperature with the appropriate clothing to wear. Corky identified ½ cup but that was the only cup measure he could identify and exhibited no skill in reading a ruler.

The FUNCTIONAL LIVING SKILLS SURVEY was completed to graphically complete personal data information on a mock job application.   He recorded his first and last name, street address, telephone number, social security, and age.   The 4 and 7 in his house number were very difficult to read.   He reported his birthday is in July.   He graphically reported his place of birth as "Earth day" but verbally reported "Akron".   Corky reported "horse" for the question regarding "race".   When questioned he still had difficulty stating his race.   For work experience Corky reported "Earth day" but verbally he reported he worked at Margaret Park School.   He did not report any hobbies or special interests.

Every six weeks or so, Marty and Corky met with the professional staff, which included someone from the Bureau of Vocational Rehabilitation, his supervisor at Goodwill, and one or two others. Marty invited me to come to one of these meetings where Corky's work performance would be evaluated. So on a December afternoon, I picked up Marty and Corky at the antique store to take them to their meeting.

"Hello, Erica Stux," Corky greeted me as he climbed into the front seat. My windshield wipers swept off the thick snowflakes that kept falling, enveloping parked cars and leaving a white blanket on the sidewalks. Traffic moved at a turtle-pace. I asked Corky if he liked the snow.

"I love it," he said emphatically. To his mom he added, "I cleaned the laundry room." Marty explained that was one of his regular chores at home.

Marty led me to the meeting room at Goodwill and introduced me to the others. We seated ourselves around a long table, Marty at one end, I on her left and Corky at the other end.

Corky's supervisor at Goodwill was a slim brunette in her mid or late twenties with a thin, angular face. A man in his early forties with thick dark hair, glasses, and an outdoor physique, a tall woman with golden-blonde hair and high cheekbones, and an older, heavier woman with a no-nonsense short haircut completed the staff.

Marlene, the Goodwill supervisor, distributed Corky's evaluation sheet and initiated discussion. Corky was fascinated by the vending machine, she related, and like a bee drawn to fragrant flowers, he headed for the machines each morning after asking for change.

Marlene stayed with Corky for his entire work shift, prompting him on proper behavior: keep working, return from your break on time, no talking, humming, or other vocalizations.

The group discussed Corky's transportation. He had been taking SCAT, a city-operated system of vans for the elderly and handicapped, but this did not always get him to work on time. Corky's mother wanted him to ride the city bus, saying the bus drivers are friendly and cooperative, and remind him where to get off. Also, she would like him to mingle with the public. The discussion led to a decision: he is to take the bus in, and SCAT out.

During the discussion, Corky sat quietly at the table, sometimes smiling to himself, nodding, or humming softly. At the beginning he announced "This is a meeting!" Later on he asked, "What time is it?" When told it was two thirty-five, he stated loudly, "The meeting is almost over."

Corky was friendly with coworkers, we were told, and greeted each by name. However, he was slow in getting his work done; it could be completed in half the time. He got easily frustrated, and could not distinguish between big mistakes and little ones. Even insignificant mistakes left him brooding for days.

Marty reminded him of something he had fussed about throughout the preceding week.

"I gotta slow down, or - I - make - mistakes," he admitted.

The professionals advised Marty to tell him, "That's the last I want to hear about that!" when he keeps fretting over something minor. She told them about making up simple tests on paper for him, like drawings of a cup with a little chip, a cup with a piece broken off, and a cup in many pieces, and asking him, "Which one is the worst?"

The discussion turned to what other kind of work Corky is capable of doing and could be assigned to. Marty mentioned his experience in dishwashing.

"How many dishes did you wash at the Catholic church?" she asked him.

"Over one hundred thousand," he replied.

"What did you like about washing dishes?" one of the professionals asked.

"The water."

"Is there another job here at Goodwill that you would like?"

"Work," he responded.

"What kind of work do you like?"

"All of 'em."

It was evident he didn't understand the question. They tried again.

"Is there anyone at Goodwill that you would like to work with?"

"Marlene," he said - his current supervisor.

Their ultimate goal was to get Corky into a community job, if an understanding employer could be found. He was happy at Goodwill, but he still needed one-on-one supervision. They recommended another four weeks at Goodwill, then possibly laundry work or dishwashing at the Sheraton Hotel, which would be a less structured environment. In the meantime, Marlene was to do less supervising and see if he could handle the limited independence.

Marty mentioned that she would like him to learn computer work. She cited his photographic memory and his ability to memorize bus schedules and the TV Guide. She would like him to be more than a laborer.

In response to her question about funding, she was assured that tax dollars would continue to pay for Corky's program. The projection was for Corky to reach a goal within six months. They all agreed that there was improvement and potential in Corky.

I took Marty back to her store and Corky to his home, although now the snow had turned into a blinding blizzard, and traffic was in gridlock. I asked him if he remembered staying with Frank, but didn't get any response. He asked to play the car radio, and tuned in his favorite station, one that played soft rock.

"Walgreens," he said as we passed that store. I stopped the car a little past his house, causing him to say, "My house back there." I realized I should let him off on his side of the street rather than making him cross over, so I turned the car around and said "Bye" as he got out.

Three weeks later, we were at a similar meeting. The problems in Corky's work record were as before: taking too long a break, and heading for the vending machines upon arrival instead of reporting for work. Also, he still got frustrated too easily.

"Do you know what happens when a worker takes too long a break?" the BVR counselor asked Corky.

"He gets fired!"

"Right!"

"I do better tomorrow," Corky promised.

They agreed that he doesn't need to have extra money with him to spend on snacks.

In four weeks, Corky was to start work in the laundry room of the Quaker Hilton Hotel. He was to fold sheets and towels - something he learned to do at Weaver School. Though at first there will be a job coach nearby, he would be working alongside others, like in a real work situation. He was told there should be little talking among the workers, so that everyone can concentrate on what he or she is doing.

"You'll be folding sheets and towels," Marty explained. "And using lots of water and soap."

"Lots of bleach," Corky added. "That I can do!"

"He likes using bleach," Marty told the others. She stood up to show a few white spots on her denim skirt. "He went overboard on the bleach here."

"If you're on your break and you still have half a candy bar to eat, what are you going to do?" the counselor asked.

"Save it till later."

"I like that answer."

I didn't see Corky again until the summer was over. He and Marty spent the summer months in Alliance at her mother's house. Starting in September, with her mother's health stabilized, they divided their time between the two homes: extended weekends in Alliance and three or four days a week in Akron.

Marty had asked me to drive her to several towns southeast of Akron to visit antique dealers. She had an item of black memorabilia that she wanted appraised and hoped eventually to sell - a large framed picture of George Primrose and Lew Dockstader, two white men that entertained in blackface at the turn of the century and into the 1920s. I had always felt that such entertainment was demeaning to blacks. But since it was part of their history, there was a demand for such items.

It was a sunny day in September when I picked up Marty and Corky. The leaves along the highway were just beginning to turn yellow and orange. The fields we passed were filled with parched corn stalks, the residue of the summer's bountiful harvest.

Corky, in the front seat, lost no time fiddling with the car radio. A light female voice filled the air with a love song.

"Aretha Franklin," he said. A little later, a male vocalist came on, and Corky announced, "Lionel Ritchie."

"See how nice Corky is dressed today?" Marty drew my attention to his black pants and white sweatshirt.

"Not tacky-macky!" Corky said.

"What's tacky-macky?"

"Cut-off jeans, pants with holes in the knees," Marty explained. "You know - grungy clothes. Corky calls it tacky-macky."

Corky burst out now and then with statements, apropos of nothing.

"It's not time for lunch yet!" (It was then ten a.m.)

"We goin' to antique stores!" All of Corky's statements seemed to end with exclamation marks.

"Lord, give me strength," he repeated several times. I recognized this as one of Marty's favorite expressions.

Marty reached from the back seat and fondled Corky's hair, and then interlaced her fingers with his.

We stopped at an ice cream stand, and Corky paid for his drink and his mother's ice cream cone. When they are out together, she lets him handle the money. A while later, he announced, "This boy starvin' to death!" We dropped him off at a Kentucky Fried Chicken while Marty and I proceeded to an antique store. Later, when we picked him up, Marty asked him what he spent on his lunch. He was reluctant to tell her. "Not ten dollars." She persisted. Finally he admitted, "Six dollars."

Our drive back was marked only by Corky's being visited by the 'Giggle-man', which Marty had told me happens occasionally. For several minutes, Corky erupted with "Hahaha, hohoho", until the 'Giggle-man' went back into hiding.

Marty was satisfied with the appraisals she received. Now all she needed was a buyer.

Chapter 24

(by Marty again)

When the movie "Rain Man" came out, tears streamed down my cheeks as I watched it. I was elated that the movie educated the public, and gave autism a human perspective. I found that people looked at Corky in a more understanding way, especially since Dustin Hoffman won an Academy Award for his portrayal of autism.

Corky has watched the movie maybe a dozen times. Once in a while, he states, "Momma, I'm autistic" and I say, "Yeah, just like the Rain Man." The more he sees that movie, the more he will perceive that he and the Rain Man are alike in many ways.

About two years after the movie's release, the real Rain Man, on whom the story was based, came to Akron to speak at Goodwill Industries. He was tall and regal in his bearing, with a large head, and a permanent smile pasted on his face. I judged him to be about 38 or 40. He was impeccably dressed in a suit and tie, and he spoke in a dignified manner. I wondered if Corky might some day end up famous like him.

At a reception following the talk, I had a long conversation with Rain Man's father. He was very encouraging to me. "Follow your instincts," he said, "and never give up." I noted with some satisfaction that Rain Man had no domestic skills whatsoever, whereas Corky can run a household quite well.

In addition to the movie, a number of books have brought autism into the public consciousness. These books document a variety of approaches in treating individual autistic children. They are for the most part success stories. But for each of these, there must be thousands whose minds and emotions are still locked up because of imperfect processing of sensory input, and whose parents and teachers are still struggling to reach them. In all the cases I read that were described by a parent, it was obvious that the autistic child was loved unconditionally. In most cases, the parent had to struggle to get appropriate help for the child.

Most inspiring are the two stories written by former autistics themselves: Temple Grandin in "Emergence - Labeled Autistic" and two books by Donna Williams, "Nobody Nowhere" and "Somebody Somewhere." Temple as a child was helped by her mother and an understanding teacher to overcome most of her unusual behaviors. A 'squeeze machine' that could give her gentle non-human hugs calmed her down. Approaching adulthood, she found that the action of walking through a special door prepared her emotionally for new experiences.

Donna Williams found security only in retreating into her own world. She learned to communicate with others by talking to herself in the presence of another person, and pretending that her words carried no emotional content at all. A severely restricted diet made Donna a calmer person.

In "There's a Boy In Here", Judy Barron and her autistic son Sean give a description and explanation, respectively, of Sean's odd behavior, which improved when he was put on the drug Ritalin.

Two very different approaches are described in "Son-Rise" by Barry Neil Kaufman and "Bobby, Breakthrough of a Special Child" by Rachel Pinney. In each of these cases, the adult entered totally into the life of the child, in the first instance imitating whatever the child did, and in the second, verbalizing whatever actions the child took. Gradually the adult then drew the child out into his environment through initiating play and talk. In both cases, the adults considered it important to assure the child that he had the adult's full attention and approval, no matter what he did. Both children outgrew their autism.

Josh Greenfeld documented life with his autistic son Noah in three separate volumes, and Jane Taylor McDonnell described the progress of her son Paul in her book "News From the Border."

From my reading, I learned there is a great variation in autistic children. The sorting out of sensory input can be quite different from child to child, and thus their behavior and emotions can be affected in a variety of ways. But all of them find it impossible to match new data with old; everything is a totally new experience. To compensate for this confusion, the child resorts to self-stimulation - rocking, spinning, finger play, etc. Not understanding the world leads to anxieties and fears that fill the child's psyche to the point that other emotions become impossible.

Most professionals agree that an autistic child should be identified and treated before age five. They generally resist catering to a child's fixations - the insistence on sameness in routine and surroundings, the meaningless body movements, etc. However, Temple Grandin recommends channeling the child's ritual fixations into productive actions, and replacing the rocking or hand flapping by external stimulations. This is what I did with Corky by having him scrub and scour and polish. Continual one-on-one contact with slow, emphatic statements on my part and words of praise at each manifestation of proper behavior helped to socialize him. Love and acceptance I certainly had, and showed it in numerous ways, right from the beginning. I always respected Corky as a unique individual, and I wanted above all to preserve his dignity.

Of course, the food supplements had a beneficial effect. I will always be grateful to Dr. Blackwood for prescribing them.

It was useless to try to explain the reasons for Corky's mannerisms to my family members, and to expect some compassion. The biggest disappointment of my life, and a source of continuing sorrow, has been the attitude of my family. We have never had any semblance of family unity. Our unspoken sentiment was 'Fare for yourself', and Corky's handicap exacerbated this attitude. It might have been different if Corky had been normal. But since, with the exception of my mother, my family members all live fairly close to me, there was no excuse for never coming over, never offering to take Corky to a movie or a restaurant. Just a hello and a pat on the back for either of us would have meant a lot.

We have family gatherings once or twice a year, usually at Thanksgiving. There are perfunctory hugs for Corky, but they are obviously fake. If Corky gets too loud or repetitious, one of my nieces, with the sensitivity of a stone, will turn to me in annoyance and ask, "Can't you make Corky shut up?" If anything were to happen to me, I think they would let Corky rot before they would lift a finger.

In my childhood I was jealous of my half-sister, who was always favored because of her lighter skin. As our lives diverged, I overcame that attitude. I developed my own talents and discovered my own worth. I never held my earlier feelings against her. I found time to babysit her children, and occasionally take them to McDonald's, or buy them gifts. Never did I receive an expression of thanks or gratitude for any of that. I now have nothing to do with her.

I lost my half-brother Dana very early. Dana was a carefree young man with a smile that could light up Mammoth Cave. He and I went to movies and shopped together when we were kids, and we remained close. I bought him classy silk shirts whenever I could afford to be generous. He graduated from high school and had ambitions to make lots of money. Women loved him, and I'm sure he had many girlfriends in his time.

Then he got mixed up with a bad crowd. One November night we got word that he had been shot in a drug-related dispute.

My mother took his death terribly hard. For the next three years she numbed her feelings with hard liquor. I was also devastated upon losing Dana.

The police finally caught up with the killer, although I felt they were not particularly diligent in investigating the case. Like other black-on-black crime, it didn't create much of a stir. Dana's killer got only six months in prison. Today he walks around free, but is a crack cocaine zombie.

I never had any contact with my father Wheatley Riley Cobb throughout my life. He was one of ten children, born in Americus, Georgia, in 1914. He attended high school in Aliquippa, Pennsylvania, and graduated from Morris Brown College in 1939 with a B.A. in social sciences. In World War II he served as a corporal and earned numerous medals, including two Bronze Stars. He was employed at American Steel Foundries as an inspector, and after his retirement he devoted much of his time to the Second Baptist Church of Alliance.

I didn't know any of this until I attended his funeral in November 1995. All I knew about him was that he had a daughter older than I, who ran away as soon as she was old enough.

I cried bitter tears at the funeral for the lost years when he could have been part of my life, but wasn't. Why didn't he ever treat me like a daughter?

My mother developed health problems in 1996, so I spent much of the summer at her house in Alliance, doing whatever I could for her. Mom is a very strong, complex person, who has had to work hard all her life. She was an excellent nurse. She assisted in surgery, passing surgical tools to the doctors, and supervised an entire nursing home during different periods of her working days.

She can be quite mean, but I love her regardless. I regret that she never treated Corky as well as she treated her first great-grandchild. Losing Dana changed her personality. She became more introspective and more critical. She is holding her own physically, although she refused to undergo kidney dialysis, as recommended by her doctor.

With Corky's other grandmother, I always enjoyed good communications, although we saw little of each other. She always had a houseful of foster children, Asian as well as black, so raising children was her main vocation. Corky and I attended her funeral in 1996. This was Corky's first funeral, and he behaved very well. Looking at his grandmother laid out in her coffin, he remarked, "She's sleeping, she's sleeping." Although he accepted the earlier death of his dog, I'm not sure whether he understood that people die too.

Chapter 25

I've had an interesting, exciting life. I've known applause, disappointments, good health, love, friendship. I've accepted Corky's condition. I've accepted the fact that I'll never have a decent black man in my life. I know I'll never perform again, and this knowledge fills me with pangs, like an all-over toothache. Taking all things together, I have made the black people's motto 'We Shall Overcome' my own.

The last two years, Corky has become very affectionate.

"I'm gonna give Momma all my kisses," he says, touching his lips gently to my forehead, cheeks, and chin.

Communication between us is so close and intricate that sometimes words are not necessary. Like two animals of the forest, we are attuned to each other's feelings. He can sense my anxiety when I'm stressed out. He brings me aspirin, and his hugs are more intense. For our tranquil times together, I put on a tape of Indian flute music, make a pot of herbal tea, light a candle, and spray cinnamon scent around the house. I can always tell when Corky is upset; his breathing becomes more labored. We have a little ritual when either one of us is agitated: We do what I call a huggy-bear dance. We hold on to each other and sway to the sounds of Indian music on a cassette tape, like two intertwined trees undulating in the wind. I say things like "This is Mommy's big boy whom Mommy loves very much…" and we continue to rock for several minutes. Corky now initiates such huggy-bear dances.

Small mistakes upset him greatly. Also dandruff. If he finds flakes of dandruff on his shoulders, he washes every brush and comb in the house, and shampoos his hair thoroughly.

Corky did not go to work at either the Sheraton or the Quaker Hilton Hotel. I took him away from the jurisdiction of the Bureau of Vocational Rehabilitation and allowed him to stay home. I wanted to give him a year of freedom, a year of no pressure to perform the jobs selected by the BVR. He hadn't been a free spirit since he first started at Weaver School at age four. He seems happy being at home, doing household chores, going shopping, and chatting with the neighbors.

Weaver School had a system of rewarding students for every correct behavior or task. One result was that Corky - and I'm sure the other students - expected a reward for everything they did.

"I swept the floor and I washed the dishes," Corky would inform me. "What do I get for that?"

"You get love and respect, and you got another good day comin'."

Corky is slowly getting to the point of developing self-respect and pride in doing a good job for its own sake, not for the promise of compensation. A gleaming kitchen floor now fills him with great pride. His regular chores include doing the dishes, making his bed, cleaning the toilet, running the sweeper, emptying the trash, and sweeping the walk outside the front door. Usually he does all this without being reminded.

In addition, he reads the newspaper, the Bible, and the dictionary. I have started him on memorizing Bible verses, which he can do readily. But he is barely beginning to understand their meaning. The Twenty-third Psalm is one that he does understand.

For entertainment, Corky has television, his music tapes, and his saxophone. Away from the house, he goes swimming and roller-skating. He also does 25 sit-ups a day. And he plans menus. However, if he had his way, he would fry chicken every single day.

He used to buy the most expensive of everything - all the well-known brands - at the supermarket and the drugstore. Now I've made him realize that he doesn't have to do that. He has become a good consumer, using discretion in his choices. He has his own money, which he spends on household and grooming items, and sometimes jazz and country-western cassette tapes. When a household item runs low, he replenishes it without being told.

Now that Corky is an accomplished young man, relatively speaking, I often wonder what was in his mind when his mommy went away for weeks at a time. I know I neglected him, and nothing will ever make up for the time together that we missed.

He still has trouble distinguishing fiction or make-believe from reality, causing him to address the actors on the TV screen. His speech has improved over the last two years, and is still improving. Sometimes he repeats himself, or slaps himself on the head in frustration when he can't get his ideas across. He is conscious of a tendency to talk too fast. His words tumble out when he gets excited.

141

When that happens, he stops and says, "I'm talking too fast. Let me say it again."

Some confusion about the proper use of pronouns remains. While Corky has a good grip of I, me, mine, the meaning of ours is only now penetrating. The concepts provided by prepositions such as near, far, or behind still give him difficulty; back and front are often interchangeable to him. "Sometimes" and "maybe" are concepts that are difficult for all autistics, to whom everything must be clear and definite - either black or white.

Only within the last two years has Corky been able to understand the difference between love and hate, friend and stranger, good person and bad person, and give and take.

Having an autistic child guarantees that you can look forward to something unusual happening every day. Recently Corky surprised me with two unexpected, strange questions: "What is a corporation?" and "What is in your stomach now?" On the other hand, he will sometimes do a task incorrectly that I thought he had mastered long ago. So I keep correcting him, even though both of us are ready to scream in frustration. And when I think "He'll never be able to do that," sooner or later he proves me wrong.

I still firmly believe that Weaver School gave him only about 25% of the education Corky was capable of absorbing. He is constantly learning more language, and I watch and listen to him in amazement. Just as he is learning, I learn something new about him every day, like when I try to explain the meaning of a word to him. The slogan at our house this year is "good listening." This is one of the hardest things for an autistic individual to do; it is so easy to tune another person out.

For reasons known only to himself, and maybe not even to himself, Corky has chosen Ed McMahon, whom he sees on TV, as a role model.

"I'm gonna cook this chicken like Ed McMahon," he will say as he prepares to fry a drumstick. Or "Today I'm gonna dress like Ed McMahon!"

Rituals that Corky still follows, after many years, are clipping coupons from the newspaper or magazines. He doesn't always have any intent to use them, but those for, say, toothpaste or soap powder he will give to me, or show me before shopping himself. Also, he still marks off each day on each of his collection of calendars. He memorizes the TV Guide every week by reading it through just once or twice.

His household methods are sometimes a little odd, like when he stacks dishes, big ones on top of little ones.

"That's gonna fall," I tell him.

"No, it ain't." And it doesn't.

He can be resourceful. When the kitchen sink developed a leak, he took two large pans to wash the dishes in, and then flushed the dishwater down the toilet.

During our summer in Alliance, Corky got hold of a gallon of white paint and decided to paint two bar stools. The stools looked attractive when he finished, but in the driveway was a huge white puddle. He had neglected to put newspaper under the stools. Miraculously, there wasn't a single white spot on his clothes or shoes.

Corky likes to put peanuts in the yard for the resident chipmunks. He has tried using tools, but doesn't know his own strength. "I'm strong, ain't I, Momma?" he will say.

New Year's Eve of 1995 we went to church, as is our custom on that day. Each individual may testify about something he or she is thankful for - recuperation from a sickness, a new baby, a successful business, etc. After several of these declarations, Corky stood up. The congregation was hushed, not knowing what to expect. One could have heard the proverbial pin drop. Corky tried to speak; his effort and concentration were obvious.

"Th-th-th-thank you, Jesus," he finally brought out.

The congregation erupted with exclamations of "Praise the Lord!" and "Glory halleluia!" They stamped their feet, they danced with arms uplifted. Everyone knew what a breakthrough this was for Corky. What we did not know, and probably will never know, was what exactly he was thankful for.

As we filed out of the building later, each person hugged Corky and me. I was touched and gratified by their support.

Corky's daily regimen of vitamins and food supplements keep him on an even keel. Every day he drinks camomile tea, two cups of valerian root tea, spring water, and catnip tea. The latter is a better tranquilizer than Dilantin or Ritalin. The valerian is a sedative; it tastes horrible, but Corky drinks it with a little lemon and honey added. One pound of valerian costs us eighteen dollars.

Among the food supplements, he takes lecithin to help his memory, vitamin B12, calcium tablets, cod liver oil, spirollina (a green barley), ginkho, and garlic. Almost all of our cooked dishes contain some garlic. Whereas I used to give Corky only organically-grown food, I now purchase a certain amount of ordinary supermarket fruits and vegetables as well.

Foods that Corky must stay away from or severely limit his intake are salt, sugar, and chocolate. This deprivation does not seem to be a problem to him, although occasionally he will sneak salt into his meals.

After a year in prison, Sammy again appeared on my doorstep, causing me to groan, "Here we go again!"

"I'm clean now," he assured me. "No cocaine. And I'm not drinkin'! See? No liquor on my breath!" Knowing his past history, I couldn't believe him.

So Sammy and Frank are still hanging around. When one leaves, the other pulls into the driveway. Each is aware of the other. Frank knows I made a mistake getting involved with Sammy. And as much as I've tried to sever the association, Sammy still insinuates himself into my life, like a bad dream that returns night after night. He knows that Frank has seniority and priority in my thoughts and actions. Jealousy gnaws at him, even though he knows that with Frank it's a platonic relationship. He has tried his best to drive Frank away. Yet he knows that if he ever harms a hair on Frank's head, he will go to jail.

Frank is still an important part of my life and of Corky's. While he doesn't live at our house any more, he drops in frequently and unexpectedly. We are a surrogate family to him. He is the only person besides myself that can discipline Corky verbally; Corky listens to him, respects him, and obeys him.

In this relationship, Frank and I are both color-blind. Frank is totally oblivious to racial differences. I am probably less so. I know that Frank is my defense in keeping harmful black men away. When a black man sees Frank hanging around, he backs off and leaves me alone.

I know if ever I should be in need of money, Frank would give it to me, no strings attached. On the other hand, if Frank should ever be sick or incapacitated and need nursing care, I'd be at his side every minute.

So I find myself trapped in the center of a triangle in which Corky, Frank, and Sammy represent the corners. I am not happy with this situation. Yet we are set in this rigid, unyielding pattern. Corky is conscious of the difference between a white man and a black one. He sees that black men have been mean to Mommy, and white men have been kind.

In recent months Sammy has become more introspective and subdued. He is taking a second look at his life as a result of his brother's suicide. Mark hanged himself in the attic of his house with a contractor's orange extension cord. I believe he was strung out on cocaine and alcohol, and perhaps feeling guilty about cheating on his wife.

Sammy has not yet come to terms with this event. Furthermore, he is still in denial over what he has done to me, which may be a good thing; if he woke up to reality, no telling what he might do, since he has absolutely no conscience. He has terrorized me so often and so brutally that the next day all I could do was sleep to get over the emotional draining. Then on the third day, I tried to catch up on what I should have done the day before, and then the accusing and the screaming would start all over again. I have dealt with this as best I can. How can a woman get rid of someone who clings to her like a leech?

1996 was a bad year for me. Between worries about Sammy, and my mother's illness, I could barely keep my head above water. Food prices have risen like the bubbles in a shaken cola. Whereas I used to spend about fifty dollars a week on groceries, now I find I must spend seventy-five.

I found a small building in Alliance that I can rent for $100 a month. It used to be a gas station once, but was abandoned long ago. I am planning to turn it into a water shop. The water supply in Alliance is not fit for drinking, and most people buy bottled water. But to purchase it, they have to drive ten or more miles. I want to provide bottled water for the people of Alliance as a convenient, steady source. I plan to buy the machine and install it in the building. I have already put gravel in the parking lot, painted the building, and laid linoleum. One room will be for the water. A second room I could make into a tiny coffee shop or a candy store. Corky can help me in this business. I already have an arrangement with a man who wants to set up a produce stand on my lot during the summer months - another source of income for me.

Weekends I have a table at the Alliance Flea Market. The Salvation Army store has specials every Monday: fifty cents an item. I purchase sweaters and other clothing there for fifty cents, recondition them, and sell them at the flea market for three or four dollars. Corky comes with me and helps me with customers. He gets right to the point with them: "Hi, whatcha wanna buy?"

Since I no longer have a car, I depend on my mother and a friend that works in Alliance to drive me back and forth.

I have gained some peace in my house by removing Sammy to Alliance. He is camping out in my building, repairing the roof and the plumbing and doing landscaping. He has a hot plate, a microwave, and a small TV set there, and I bring him food once or twice a week. He also does odd jobs around town to survive. He seems content to be there, I gain free labor, and I know he cannot disturb Corky when Corky remains in Akron.

I realize now that I was blinded by Sammy's multitude of talents. I didn't stop to analyze his character, which was molded in a family with absolutely no warmth or love.

The city of Akron is going to raze the block in which I have my antique store, to make way for a parking lot. I am to receive a sum of money to move my store. But if I decide not to move it, the money is mine, to dispose of as I please.

So, one way or another, I will manage to survive, and to provide for Corky.

One of the best choices I ever made was to raise Corky without medication, and see him overcome his condition and grow up into a fine, dignified gentleman. The pain, the suffering, the disappointments and sacrifices cannot measure up to the glory of what I've accomplished with Corky. For everything bad, something good has happened.

What I want for Corky's future is to find a foundation that will underwrite further education for him. I would like to have a private tutor to give him computer training. I would like to have a private physical education coach, a private language tutor, a nutritionist to prepare Corky's meals, and a private music teacher. And I would like to have a private swimming pool where Corky can swim each morning. Decent health insurance to take the place of his medical card would make life easier for him also. Lastly, I want a double cemetery plot, bought and paid for, as a final resting place for me and Corky.

All these services are expensive, of course, and I will never be able to afford them. But Corky deserves the best. I owe him the opportunity to become a successful human being. I want him to have a peaceful, sheltered life, to find things for himself that are gratifying. I want a place for him to live that has security, tranquility, and beauty. And perhaps some day he might even gain a nice girlfriend. If anything should happen to me, I know that Frank and Robert Robey and Dwaine Poteete will be there to look after Corky. If I know he is loved and taken care of, my mind and soul will be at rest, and I can die in peace.

About the Author

Originally trained as a chemist, Erica Stux began writing when her children were young. She has had many poems and prose pieces for children published, as well as adult humor and light verse. Her books include a novel *Landlady*, poetry booklets, a biography of women in the arts, and a biography of author and abolitionist Lydia Maria Child. She especially enjoys writing about nature for children. Most of her life was spent in Ohio, but she now lives in Chatsworth, California, with her husband Bill Shore.